Live
Rich

ALSO BY STEPHEN M. POLLAN AND MARK LEVINE

Die Broke

Live Rich

*Everything You Need to Know
to Be Your Own Boss,
Whomever You Work For*

Stephen M. Pollan and Mark Levine

HarperBusiness
A Division of HarperCollinsPublishers

HarperCollins books may be purchased for educational, business, or sales promotional use. For information please write: Special Markets Department, HarperCollins Publishers, Inc., 10 East 53rd Street, New York, NY 10022.

FIRST EDITION

Designed by Elina D. Nudelman

Library of Congress Cataloging-in-Publication Data
Pollan, Stephen M.
    Live rich : everything you need to know to be your own boss, whoever you work for /
Stephen M. Pollan, Mark Levine. — 1st ed.
        p.   cm.
    ISBN 0-88730-935-6
    1. Finance, Personal.   I. Levine, Mark, 1958–   .   II. Title.
HG179.P555435   1998
332.024—dc21   98-39060

98 99 00 01 02 ❖/RRD 10 9 8 7 6 5 4 3 2 1

This book is dedicated to
Arthur Levine
and
Max Staller
and to my brother Erwin,
who taught me the secrets of living rich

Contents

Acknowledgments

We'd like to thank our agent, Stuart Krichevsky, for helping us set a goal, and then having the faith to stick with us for the ten years it took to reach it.

Thanks to our editor, Adrian Zackheim, for helping us finally see the individual trees lost in the forest of our own ideas.

Thanks to our wives, Corky Pollan and Deirdre Martin Levine, for showing us what living rich really means.

Thanks to the clients of Stephen Pollan, P.C., for letting us draw on their lives and experiences in order to help others.

Thanks to Jane Morrow for letting us tap into her memories and observations.

Thanks to John Koten and Laurence Hooper for helping us develop and refine our contrarian instincts.

Thanks to Gary Ambrose, Shelly M. Greenwald, Richard Koenigsberg, Mike Powers, Stuart Rosenblum, Gabriella Rowe, Kenny Tillman, and Emmanuel Zimmer for letting us borrow their expertise.

Thanks to Randy S. Newman, Anthony Scamurra, Abraham Romano, Craig Kessler, and Liz Petschauer for their continued support.

Finally, we'd like to thank the following experts whose advice and writings were among the varied threads we needed to help people weave their own rich lives: Joel Best, William Bridges, Timothy Butler,

Susan Campbell, D. Lee Carpenter, Stan Davis, Alan Dershowitz, Paul and Sarah Edwards, Martha Friedman, Herb Goldberg, Adolf Guggenbühl-Craig, James Hillman, Sara Horowitz, Neil Howe, Robert Hughes, Susan Jeffers, Wendy Kaminer, John Kotter, Landon Y. Jones, Richard Leider, Robert T. Lewis, Henry Clay Lindgren, Russell A. Lockhart, Terri Lonier, Stanton Peele, Tom Peters, William Strauss, Charles Sykes, James Waldroop, Bob Waterman, and Bernie Zilbergeld.

Part I

The Live Rich Philosophy

Buying Your Own Freedom $\quad$ 1

Live rich. When you come down to it, isn't that what we all want? To live the life of our dreams?

For some, living rich means owning a magnificent, well-appointed home, perhaps on the beach. For others, it's being able to buy whatever they want, for themselves or others, without worrying about the price tag. Still others, myself included, think it means traveling the world, first class (at least business class), and staying in four-star hotels. Creative individuals dream of being able to write or sing or paint or sculpt without worrying about paying their rent. The spiritually motivated want to be able to spend time getting closer to God, whether it takes the form of meditative prayer or feeding the hungry. Everyone has a personal vision of what goes into a rich life.

There's one common element, however: freedom. Look at all the different dreams of a rich life, and you'll see every single one is based on having the freedom to do whatever you want to do. Living rich is having the freedom to live on the beach, to buy whatever you want, to travel the world, to create art for art's sake, or to spend your life in service to God. Living rich is also having the freedom to set aside your fears and seize the reins of your life. To live rich is to be free, and to be free is to live rich.

Living rich isn't the same as *being* rich. No one whose mind is healthy really equates a rich life with being wealthy. Money in and of itself isn't what we want. But what we *do* want may be able to be purchased with money.

Obviously it takes money to buy that house on the beach, to purchase all those lovely things, and to afford first-class travel. But it also takes money to be able to do nonmaterial things, like create art or lead a life of prayer. All of us, even artists and contemplatives, live in a capitalist world. It takes money to obtain the necessities of life—food, clothing, and shelter. That money comes from either our own work or the work of others.

Someone, somewhere—perhaps a spouse or a parent—is working so the idealistic artist can spend time painting. And someone, somewhere—perhaps some wealthy materialist paying $10 for a jar of preserves—is working so the devoted Trappist monk can spend all his waking hours at prayer.

You might not be comfortable acknowledging it, but money plays a big part in whether you're able to live rich, to be free.

So far, it seems that living rich would be pretty simple. Since you're the one who decides exactly what living rich means, and since money—in one way or another—is what enables you to pursue that dream, all you need to do is get enough money to fulfill that dream. But if that's the case, if it's really that simple, how come so few of us actually live rich?

FROM DIE BROKE TO LIVE RICH

Two years ago I wrote a book called *Die Broke*. It advocated treating assets as resources to be used, in whatever way you choose, during your lifetime, rather than as treasures to be hoarded and passed on after your death. I wrote it in response to what I saw in my own consulting practice. I'm an lawyer and financial adviser on Manhattan's Upper East Side. My practice is small, but offers a wide range of services: I help my clients with everything from their personal finances to their careers and businesses. I offer very personalized service. That's why I was deeply affected by what I saw happening just a few short years ago.

I saw my clients diligently follow all the rules of personal finance they'd been taught (by me as well as by other authors and advisers), yet still find themselves falling short of their goals and dreams. In my search to help them, I discovered it wasn't my clients who were failing, it was the system. They were simply following a misguided philosophy and outdated rules designed for an economic environment that had disappeared.

After a great deal of thought and research, I came up with what I thought was a new, more workable, more effective philosophy of personal finance, along with a set of simple, pragmatic rules: Quit today, pay cash, don't retire, and die broke.

The response to *Die Broke* exceeded my wildest dreams. With all due modesty, I knew my philosophy and advice on personal finance worked. After all, I see the positive results every day in my office. However, I didn't realize the extent to which my clients' financial fears and frustrations were echoed in the general public.

Admittedly, my client base isn't a cross section of the American population. While my clients come from a variety of ethnic, social, cultural, and religious backgrounds, most are middle- and upper-income New Yorkers between the ages of twenty-five and fifty. I didn't know so many people of other ages and from other places would find the *Die Broke* philosophy helpful in eliminating the frustrations they felt with their personal finances. I suppose, whatever else you can say, positive or negative, about New York baby boomers, one thing is clear: They are on the cutting edge of social and financial trends. The success of *Die Broke* and the realization that my clients' fears and hopes were no different from those of the rest of the population has led me to offer the advice from the other part of my consulting practice.

I take, for lack of a better word, a comprehensive approach to my clients' financial lives. As I mentioned, I get very involved in their world. Rather than working with them on just one element, say their investments, I treat their money and their circumstances as a mosaic of various pieces that make up what I call the business of living. *Die Broke* dealt with one half of the business of living: spending money. This book, *Live Rich*, deals with the other half of the business of living: earning money.

THE STORY OF EDDIE ZOLLMAN

The first time I met Eddie and Anita Zollman* he was a nervous wreck and she was very pregnant. Eddie, a forty-two-year-old Alan

---

*I have changed the names and some of the details of my clients' stories throughout this book to protect their privacy.

Alda look-alike, was a political reporter at one of New York City's daily newspapers. Anita was a thirty-six-year-old art teacher, then on maternity leave while expecting the birth of their first child. They had come to me for help in finding a new apartment. At the time, they were renting a one-bedroom apartment in Brooklyn. It was cramped for the two of them; it would be impossible for three.

The first thing I did was ask Eddie and Anita about their income. Anita had been earning approximately $40,000 a year as a teacher. But it was clear after just a few minutes of discussion that she had no intention of going back to work until the baby they were expecting was in elementary school. That meant they'd need to rely on Eddie's salary for at least five years. He was earning $50,000 a year. That was more than Eddie said he'd ever dreamed he'd make. Back when he was a cub reporter fresh out of Syracuse University's journalism school, he was earning $12,000 covering suburban zoning board meetings. When he and Anita had two incomes and no children, a combined $90,000 income was fine. Granted, they didn't save anything, but they lived quite well, thank you. Now, however, $50,000 didn't look like it would be enough for them to keep a roof over their heads, and the head of their baby, let alone buy a larger place.

I started quizzing Eddie about this job. He was very well known in journalism circles. A serious, sober, hardworking reporter, he was (and is) respected for his ability to both dig up and write stories. Newspaper journalism isn't a high-paying field, and Eddie's attitude didn't help matters. He had never gone in and asked for a raise. Instead he simply counted on getting an annual 3 to 4 percent increase on the anniversary of his being hired. When I broached the idea of pushing for more, he said, "That just isn't done." Newspapers in New York City weren't "making money," he stressed. He was "lucky just to have this job."

"I guess you must really like what you're doing," I said.

"Actually," he responded, "I hate my job."

"I HATE MY JOB"

I hear those four words, or their entrepreneurial equivalent ("I hate what I do") at least once a week. They come from clients of all ages and economic levels—the established single professional woman earning $200,000 plus, the married middle manager in his prime earning between $50,000 and $100,000, and the young ad agency staffer earning between $25,000 and $50,000. All of them, despite their admitted hatred for their job, career, or business, are working harder than they've ever worked in their lives. They're starting earlier and working later than ever before. There isn't a weekend when they're not taking work home. Even when they're on "vacation" they stay in touch with the office. Their families and social lives are playing second fiddle to their work lives. They're devoting almost all their time and energy to something they say they hate.

Saying "I hate my job" or "I hate what I do" is like saying "I'm fine" when someone asks how you're doing. It's a reflexive phrase that's so general it's meaningless. If you were at a party and casually said to someone you'd just met, "I hate my job," he'd rhetorically ask, "Who doesn't." Then he'd either walk away, looking for someone more interesting, or immediately steer the conversation to El Niño. Since my clients are paying me for my time and advice I'm not so quick to walk away when faced with such innocuous statements. And the weather is a serious subject for me—I have one of those digital weather stations at home. So instead of shrugging off the remark, I probe for specifics. I ask, "Why do you hate your job?" or "Why do you hate what you do?" And after a bit of lawyerly pressure I usually get to the heart of the matter.

Many clients reveal they're "not making enough money." Those who are employees often admit to feelings of insecurity and vulnerability— "I could be let go tomorrow"—or a sense that they have no future—"I'm stuck on the corporate ladder." Entrepreneurs, on the other hand, often say the business has lost its appeal: "The business isn't working for me, I'm working for it." Nearly all, regardless of whom they work for, say, "I don't love what I'm doing" or "My work just isn't rewarding."

Of course, there are some people who come to see me who don't hate their jobs. In fact, these clients generally say they "love" their work. While there may be things about their company or business they find annoying and frustrating—perhaps the office politics or the lack of financial reward—they find the work they're doing emotionally, even spiritually, rewarding. These clients usually come to me thinking they just need a "tune-up" rather than a total overhaul. They're wrong.

They're lucky to have found work that's emotionally rewarding. I know that because I share their luck. I find my own work very gratifying. However, loving your work isn't a blessing; actually it's a trap. Love truly is blind. People who feel strongly about their work often fail to see dangers or problems with their jobs or businesses because they're infatuated with their work. Unfortunately, love of work is always unrequited. No company and no business has the capacity to love you back, no matter how devoted you are to what you're doing. Having crushed your illusions, let me give you a chance to recover by returning to Eddie Zollman.

Eddie Zollman combined both problems. While he loved his work he hated his job. He was scared of being laid off and thought that, despite his being respected in the field, his future wasn't secure. Eddie was a political reporter, but not an office politician, and therefore didn't see himself moving up to a management position at the paper. He was also burned out. Most important, however, he felt he simply wasn't making enough money. Yet he didn't see how he could get any more. "There just isn't any money in journalism," he said, "but at my age, I can't afford to shift professions. I'm stuck."

Once I get a specific answer, even one as pessimistic as Eddie's, I offer the client my congratulations. Most clients think I'm being facetious, but I'm not. I can be a wise guy with my friends but I'm never facetious with clients. I offer my congratulations because often the hardest part of solving overwhelming problems is specifically defining what's wrong. Once that's done, finding a solution is easy: You just have to update your attitude toward work to reflect the current environment, and learn some simple new survival rules.

TRULY WORK FOR YOURSELF

For all intents and purposes we have been in the twenty-first century for years. (Just as an aside, I think when historians look back on our times they'll cite the invention and proliferation of the personal computer as the point when the twentieth century ended and the twenty-first began.) Despite our living in a new world, our attitudes toward work are based on twentieth-century, and in some cases nineteenth-century, principles.

I'll get into all this in greater detail throughout this book, but for now let me just say that the assumptions and expectations most of us bring to our work lives are outdated and self-defeating.

(This shouldn't be news to readers of *Die Broke*, who learned that most common attitudes toward personal finance are similarly based on outdated twentieth-century principles and rules that need to be replaced with updated twenty-first-century attitudes and maxims.)

Most of us have been taught and encouraged to believe that:

If you do your work you'll keep your job.

If you do your work *well* you'll be promoted.

If you keep your job you'll get regular pay raises.

If you get promoted you'll get a sizable pay raise.

If you're loyal to the company the company will be loyal to you.

An entrepreneur's success is directly tied to his company's success.

For you to be happy your work must be meaningful.

In fact, none of these assumptions is true. There's no justice in the workplace . . . and there never was.

People can't count on paternalistic employers . . . and they never could.

The days of automatic pay raises are gone . . . in part because they were never here.

There's no such thing as corporate loyalty . . . and there never was.

The interests of a business and its owner are not identical . . . and they never should have been.

And, while deriving self-actualization from work is wonderful, it is less likely than ever before—it was always a long shot. Pursuing it, or trying to maintain it, at the expense of more basic needs is dangerous.

To many of my clients, and probably to you, the first five points aren't news. Tens of thousands of layoffs have lifted the scales from your eyes. The final two points, on the other hand, usually come as a shock and are greeted with resistance and denial. But give me a chance. By the end of the first part of this book I think you'll be convinced, just as clients are convinced after an hour or two in my office.

I believe we need to abandon these assumptions and expectations and adopt a new attitude toward work. We need to *truly* work for ourselves. That sounds simpler than it is.

Just because you're self-employed doesn't mean you're working for yourself. Far from it. Few entrepreneurs *really* work for themselves. Deep down, most work for someone or something else, whether it's their company, their employees, their parents, or their spouse and children.

I know this firsthand, not just by learning it from my entrepreneur clients, but because, even though I've been self-employed most of my adult life, I've only recently truly started working for myself.

While I'll be using examples drawn from my clients' lives throughout this book, as I did in *Die Broke*, I think it's only fair to also talk about my own life. After all, I'll be asking you, as I ask my clients, to explore your psyche to determine your own needs. You have a right, therefore, to hear the results of my own exploration.

I became a lawyer not because I loved the law, but because I wanted to please my parents. I grew up in a solidly middle-class Jewish home in the Bronx. My father sold milk and eggs and my mother worked at home, raising me and my two siblings. My parents (both of whom are still alive, by the way) wanted their children to do better than they had done. They encouraged us to "succeed." A newspaper of the time—I forget which one it was—used to run a small daily profile of a "successful man." My father used to cut that item out of the newspaper every single morning and put it on my pillow at night so I would read it before I went to bed. I was a good student, and after a couple of years of college I was offered a scholarship to law school. In my parents' eyes (and admittedly mine at the time) there was no question about what to do. I left college, took the scholarship, and became a lawyer. (It took another forty years for me to finally go back and get that bachelor's degree I had tossed aside.)

When I graduated law school, rather than entering a firm, I struck out on my own. Partly that was because of my own innate entrepreneurial streak, but it was also because I wanted to make as much money as I could as quickly as I could. Why? To prove myself to my in-laws, particularly my father-in-law. He was a very wealthy, successful man who, I felt, looked down on me and thought his daughter— my wife, Corky—had married someone unworthy. (Now, many years later, I've come to view him less critically and realize he was in many ways a positive role model for me.)

I had to ask for his help to buy our first house, and he always acted as if the house was actually his, not ours. He used to come to visit us in our little Levittown-style house in Farmingdale, Long Island, and walk around, knocking on the walls, inspecting "his" house. As a result, I was driven to get out from his shadow and prove I could provide for his daughter and his grandchildren. I did.

I launched a successful law office and real estate development business, became president of an American Stock Exchange–listed venture capital fund, and became the real estate specialist for National Westminster Bank. But, in retrospect, I wasn't working for myself. It was only after I contracted tuberculosis and was forced to live for two years on my disability insurance benefits that I started truly working for myself.

One day I was sitting in my bathrobe in our apartment on Park Avenue in Manhattan (I always joke that I caught tuberculosis on Park Avenue) when someone rang the doorbell. It was my friend Greg Roy, a teacher and struggling actor. He was frantic because the telephone company was threatening to cut off his service for not paying his bill. I told him not to worry. I called the telephone company pretending to be him and negotiated a payment plan with them that Greg could afford and that would allow him to keep his telephone service. When I hung up Greg was stunned. "You have to tell people about how to do this," he said. And from that moment on, I have. I started a personal consulting business that helps people take charge of their financial and work lives. And it's only after starting *that* business that I've truly been working for myself.

Just as self-employment is not a guarantee of working for yourself, so employment is not an insurmountable obstacle to it. You can *truly* work for yourself and still get a paycheck. Once again, let me tell you about my experience.

Because I have spent most of my life as an entrepreneur, I have to go back quite a few years to find a "job" I held in which I was truly working myself. I have to go so far back, in fact, that the job and the place I worked no longer exist.

When I was going to law school I supported myself by working at the drugstore located on the first floor of the Barbizon Hotel for Women. This was one of the resident hotels for women that used to be quite common in Manhattan. For some reason, at the time it wasn't considered proper for single women of a certain "class" to live in a coed apartment building.*

The drugstore downstairs not only sold prescriptions, cosmetics, toi-

---

*At the Barbizon, men were not permitted above the second floor. Of course I occasionally broke this rule, but only in emergencies when I had to deliver chocolates to needy diabetic residents.

letries, and sundries, but had a lunch counter. After working there for a couple of years I worked my way up to being the soda jerk. This was a job where I was truly working for myself. I may have been collecting a paycheck signed by Nat Scollar, who owned the drugstore, but I was satisfying my own real needs behind that lunch counter. There I was, a young, single, middle-class Jewish boy, struggling to go to school and make ends meet, and eager to move up in the world. And every day I was able to work in a position where I had a great deal of autonomy, was paid a living wage (if you included the tips), and got the chance to meet, talk to, and wait on young, well-to-do, single women. Those were my real needs at that time.

In all seriousness, that's what truly working for yourself really means. It has nothing to do with who signs your paycheck. It means working to satisfy *your own real needs*, not just perceived needs, and not the needs of someone or something else.

You're not working for yourself if you're pursuing a profession to please your parents or a teacher. You're not working for yourself if you're always putting the needs of your boss and coworkers before your own. You're not working for yourself if you're in a particular job because you think it pleases your spouse. You're not working for yourself if you're satisfying needs you "think" you should have—whether it's a owning a suburban split-level or holding a job feeding the hungry. You're not working for yourself if your goal is satisfying your company's needs. You're only truly working for yourself when you're satisfying your own (not someone else's) real (not just perceived) needs.

EDDIE ZOLLMAN'S OWN REAL NEEDS

I told Eddie and Anita Zollman about my father-in-law, the Barbizon Hotel, and my theory of truly working for yourself. At first Eddie was skeptical—most journalists instinctively are when they hear something new. Anita, trained as an artist and teacher, was more open to the concept. Counting on her support, I suggested Eddie think about it before our next meeting, at which we planned to go over their real estate options.

A week later a much less nervous Eddie Zollman showed up at my office. Anita couldn't make it that day since she wasn't feeling well, but Eddie did bring along a message from her. She said that for her, at this time, truly working for herself meant spending all her time raising the baby she was carrying. I wasn't surprised. But I was taken aback when Eddie turned to himself. "I've realized that to truly work for myself, I need to make more money," he said with the zeal of the newly converted.

Eddie told me that he had gone into journalism in part to please his parents. They were ultra-liberal Irish Catholics from Boston—I suppose today you'd say they were into liberation theology. Journalism was, in their eyes, a way to serve society. Money was never considered important in Eddie's family. In fact, it was seen as corrupting. Eddie still shared much of his parents' political ideology, but when faced with his own job dissatisfaction and the imminent arrival of his child, he'd come to realize money did make a difference to him. Eddie had seen enough of the industry to realize journalism wasn't the sacred trust his parents had thought and he'd once believed. Though he still loved digging up a good story and writing a powerful lead, he had burned out on the job of being a journalist. He said providing for his child was more important to him than anything else. As a result, he told me he'd decided his goal was to make more money, and if that meant leaving the newspaper, he'd do it. With that, I told him we should put his and Anita's apartment hunt on hold. Instead, I suggested, let's concentrate on getting more money.

I had him start by making networking telephone calls to people inside and outside the newspaper business. His pitch was that, with a child on the way, he was interested in finding out whether people thought there might be other career options open to him. A series of telephone calls and meetings led to his getting an interview with a magazine publishing entrepreneur. This gentleman was looking to launch a new publication for politicians and their staffs. He wanted Eddie to come on board as a contributing editor . . . at a salary of $70,000 . . . with a two-year contract.

Eddie was torn. He definitely wanted the higher salary. But he wasn't comfortable with the magazine entrepreneur. He simply didn't trust him. Besides, he knew that startups were risky—he could be out of work within six months. I told him there was middle ground between accepting and rejecting this offer: gentle coercion. I had Eddie schedule an emergency meeting with his managing editor at the newspaper. I told him to say he needed to ask his boss's advice. He went to his long-time editor and said he had a terrible problem. Out of the blue he had gotten this call offering him a job for $20,000 more than he was making at the newspaper. With a baby on the way money was a big issue. Still, Eddie stressed, he loved the newspaper and really wanted to stay. What should he do? he asked. The managing editor came back to Eddie two days later with a three-year contract . . . at a salary of $75,000. After going over the details with me, Eddie signed the deal.

Almost as important as the added money was the change in Eddie's attitude toward work and himself. He realized that by focusing on what he really wanted, and taking charge of the situation, he could achieve far more than he ever thought.

NEW RULES FOR LIVING RICH

You can develop an understanding of your own true needs through soul searching, self-analysis, prayer, meditation . . . whatever method you'd like.

No road to the truth is any better or any quicker than any other. Just as we each have our own needs, we also each have our own best path toward discovering those needs. There's a wonderful Buddhist proverb that says: "Better your own dharma [path] badly done than the dharma of another." I wish I could help you uncover those truths, but I'm not a psychotherapist. (In fact I'm quite troubled by the direction therapy has taken these days, as you'll see in Chapters 2 and 4.) I'm a financial therapist. While I can't help you uncover your true needs, I can tell you about how some clients of mine uncovered theirs, and I can show you how I helped them meet their needs.

Remember: No needs are any "better" or "nobler" than any others. The individual who pursues wealth can turn around and donate a great deal to charity. And the person who serves her community in a low-paying but "meaningful" job could be forcing her family to do without things.

Don't worry. Adopting this new attitude toward work won't leave you rudderless in the stormy seas of the twenty-first-century workplace. There are new rules, or better yet, maxims, that you can apply to your life, replacing those outdated assumptions and expectations.

The first three maxims apply to everyone. They are:

Make money.

Don't grow, change.

Take charge.

And then entrepreneurs and employees each have their own fourth maxim, either:

Create Yourself.com (entrepreneurs).

Or:

Become a mercenary (employees).

I'll fully explore each of these maxims in subsequent chapters, but let me just briefly explain them.

Make Money

Sounds simple. We all want to make money. Then how come so few of us feel like we have enough? I think it's because, for a variety of psychological and cultural reasons, we subconsciously feel there's something wrong with making money. We believe money is somehow crass, venal, and dirty. That's ludicrous. I don't think there's anything wrong with money—in fact, there's a lot right with it. To survive and thrive in the twenty-first century you need to make the acquisition of money a high priority.

That doesn't mean money must be your exclusive goal—although there's nothing wrong with that. It means that in our capitalist society money is a necessary tool to achieve happiness and to satisfy work-related needs . . . whatever they are.

Money in and of itself can do nothing. When the paper dollar stopped being backed by silver, and when coins were no longer worth their weight in precious metal, money lost its intrinsic value. But it's extrinsically invaluable. Taken as a tool, money can do almost anything. It may not be able to buy you happiness, but it can buy most of the things that bring happiness, including health to some degree. Certainly the lack of money can make you miserable.

The search for work that's fulfilling emotionally is noble but quixotic, especially today. I'm not saying it's impossible, just improbable. And pursing such a utopian mission can lead to frustration.

If you've been lucky enough to find gratifying work, that's wonderful. But I don't think it's enough. At least it's not enough for me or for most of my clients. You can't let your emotional satisfaction get in the way of a vital truth: Work is the only area of your life that has the power to generate money for you. Gratification, on the other hand, can come from every other area of your life: hobbies, church, family, exercise, you name it. But none of those can give you the money that work can. Your goal for work should be to make money. If you can make sufficient money doing something you find emotionally gratifying, offer a prayer of thanks. You're one of the few. But if you're not generating sufficient income, please don't let your love of what you're doing blind you to your need to find another way to make money.

It's only the baby boom generation that has ever really had the hubris to try to find work that is both emotionally gratifying and financially rewarding. And for a while it seemed they might be able to achieve it. But economic changes slammed shut that window of opportunity. I don't think that was a bad thing, however. With self-actualization only a faint hope, you can now focus on what really matters about work—making money—and pursue fulfillment in areas of your life where you have a greater chance of finding it.

Remember: Work is the area in your life that gives you the best chance to earn money. And it's the other areas of your life that give you the best chance at self-actualization. You can help the world by volunteering. You can be creative through a hobby. You can get a sense of purpose and a feeling of joy by caring for your family. You can be spiritually uplifted at a house of worship. My advice is to render unto work the things that are work's—the ability to make money—and render unto God, and family, and community the things that are God's, the family's, and the community's—the ability to provide psychological, emotional, and spiritual fulfillment.

Don't Grow, Change

It's obvious the implied contract that once bound workers and their employers has been torn to shreds. There's no longer any guarantee that if you do your job you'll keep it, or that if you do your job well you'll get a raise or promotion. There's also no longer any reward for length of service or sacrifices for the company. The skilled bookkeeper who has been with the company for twenty years is as likely, perhaps more likely, to be laid off as the neophyte clerk who started yesterday. The sales executive who moves his family across the country when the company suggests a transfer can be out of work before he finishes unpacking his golf clubs. In the twenty-first century there's no career or job ladder to climb, there's no loyalty, and there's no justice. All the signs and markers on the path to career success have been removed. You're on your own with your new attitude, new rules, and your innate sense of direction to guide you.

Similarly, there's no longer a set pattern of business. Small companies used to get a foothold by carving out a niche in an existing market and then climb by increasing their market share. In the process they grew in size and scope. Some brought more of the functions they relied on in-house. Others opened new outlets in new geographic areas. In both cases, staff and plant grew. In this way a one- or two-person operation could become a $1 million corporation with a staff of hundreds, if not thousands.

Yet for the past decade large, established companies have been doing the exact opposite. In reaction (some would say overreaction) to the new economic environment, corporations are downsizing and focusing on their core functions. Meanwhile, most small business people are still thinking of growth or expansion.

Rather than focusing on climbing a ladder or growing a company, you must financially and emotionally invest solely in yourself instead. As an employee or entrepreneur you should try to increase your own skills and do things that increase your income, marketability, and, most of all, profitability. Please don't let yourself be detoured by psychic benefits like corner offices, impressive titles, larger facilities, or bigger staffs. What counts is that your company or job is satisfying your real needs and making you money.

Try to stop doing things that interfere with those goals. Don't put down roots in either a company or a business if you can help it. Physically as well as emotionally you'll be better off if you're able to pull up stakes and move quickly. If you're an employee that may mean living, to the greatest extent possible, out of your briefcase, keeping your résumé in circulation, and becoming a regular at networking functions and organizations, not just in your industry, but in other industries and in your community. If you're an entrepreneur that could mean not renting space if you can avoid it. It might mean working from home if you can, or selling your products via the Internet or a catalog. It might even mean not hiring *any* employees, and using temps and freelancers instead. For me, at least, it means outsourcing every function other than my own personal specialty. For everyone it means focusing on your own personal bottom line, whether you're an employee or an entrepreneur.

Your bank balance is what counts, not the company's coffers or your business's books.

In the twenty-first century if we're going to flourish we all have to get used to being ready to move in any direction. It's going to be very difficult to earn money by doggedly following a prescribed pattern, whether it's climbing the next rung on an organizational chart or increasing your market share by 10 percent. I think employees should now look for opportunities rather than promotions. I tell my entrepreneur clients to look for new markets rather than increasing market shares. If you're an employee you should be looking for another project—inside or outside your present company—or an opportunity to become an entrepreneur. If you're already an entrepreneur you should be looking for the next business to start, the next product or service to offer—or perhaps even an opportunity to work on a project inside a company.

Take Charge

In the twenty-first century you can no longer be reactive. You need to take charge of your own life to live rich. You may think you're already taking charge, but I'll wager you're still reacting to others, whether they're your superiors, customers, clients, or suppliers. Are you waiting for a raise or promotion or a new project? Are you waiting for payment or for customers to come to you or for suppliers to let you know about new products? That's not going to cut it in the twenty-first century. Instead you must become positively proactive and start taking measured risks.

The secret to doing that is to break free of the culture of victimization that has taken over America and to overcome the fears that are freezing you in place. You must stop blaming others for your situation, take responsibility for your successes and failures, and take charge of your life. You may have had strict parents. You may even have had abusive parents. You may suspect you're being discriminated against. Or you may in fact be discriminated against. It doesn't matter. In the final analysis you are responsible for your own success or failure. You are the only one who can keep you from living rich.

If you're like most of my clients you do things to yourself you'd never let others, even those whom you've blamed, get away with today. You let self-centered fears keep you from taking the actions necessary to thrive. You need to get out of your own head, stop blaming others, stop judging your success or comparing yourself to others, and start taking forward steps. The worst possible result of an action is seldom as bad as you imagine it in your head.

Blame and fear freeze you in place, and the status quo spells doom in the twenty-first century. You have to be courageous, to raise your sails, to take risks, to set goals and priorities, to stop measuring yourself.

You need to wake up to life and cherish each and every day. You need to develop the courage to take responsibility for yourself, to realize that taking risks isn't the same as gambling, and to accept that life isn't ad hoc—you have to set goals and priorities. Most of all, you have to stop living in the past and worrying about the future, and instead live rich in the present.

Create Yourself.com

You are not your business. Your business is nothing more than an avenue for profit. It should not be an entity in and of itself. Treat your business as a separate entity, and you start doing things for it rather than it doing things for you. You start worrying about how it's doing rather than how you're doing. You start focusing on its growth rather than your wallet. You start thinking of its image, rather than your lifestyle. You start worrying about its future rather than your present. Your business exists solely to satisfy your own real needs. It should have no needs of its own . . . at least none you should care about.

Instead I suggest you create your own personal company, which I call Yourself.com. Yourself.com isn't the particular business you're in at the moment, it's the work or commercial aspect of your life. Yourself.com is the vehicle through which you can start or buy new profitable businesses, kill off or sell old ones, or perhaps even form a joint venture with another organization or an employer for a time. What's key is that Yourself.com never has any agenda other than your personal needs and wants. Just as superinvestor Warren Buffet has Berkshire Hathaway that represents his (and his shareholder partners) financial interests, so you should have your own Yourself.com. It's the infrastructure for all your commercial efforts, the common thread that ties together all your efforts to make money.

Become a Mercenary

Workplace pundits are offering hundreds of suggestions—some savvy, some silly—about how employees can deal with the changing economy and come out on top. Many, including myself in *Die Broke*, have urged employees to think of themselves like free agent athletes. I think the free agent analogy works for those who have specific talents that remain in demand and who can negotiate pay based on their past performance. But I believe there's a better, if less modern, role model that *all* employees can emulate: the condottiere of the Renaissance.

The condottiere were soldiers for hire who had a personal code of conduct, who were loyal (as long as they were paid), and who readily joined into units with other professional soldiers. Perhaps you know them better by the name they were given in England: free lances. The condottiere were answerable ultimately only to themselves, responsible for their own security and safety, for their own growth of skills, their own savings, their own futures. They were always looking for the next battle to fight.

BUT WHAT ABOUT LIVING RICH?

In all honesty I never set out to write a book on how to live rich. No client ever came into my office and asked, "Stephen, how do I live rich?" And since all my advice, and all my writing, is based on the practical needs of clients and readers, I never thought I'd pursue such a lofty, ethereal goal. But sometimes we find wisdom in the strangest places, and when we're not even looking for it. It was only after speaking with, of all people, Eddie and Anita Zollman that I realized the truth.

It was five years after our first meeting, and Eddie and Anita and their daughter, Courtney, were now living in a two-bedroom condo that we'd found in Fort Lee, New Jersey. Courtney was about to go to school, and Anita was considering going back to work as an art teacher. Eddie's second contract with the newspaper was about to expire, and he and I were simultaneously negotiating a third one, and looking for other opportunities. I told them I was working on a follow-up book to *Die Broke*, a volume about my philosophy of truly working for yourself. I asked if I could use their story, slightly camouflaged, in this new book. They agreed, and we started talking about the effects of applying my philosophy.

Many clients had told me how my approach had helped them become happier about their work. Others said they'd become more satisfied with their finances and their economic circumstances. Some even said they'd achieved a measure of peace and serenity. But it was Eddie who brought it all together for me. When I asked him what he got from following my career advice he looked up for a moment, as if to get an answer from heaven, then looked me in the eye and said, "Not only can I tell you the result of following your philosophy, but I have the perfect title for your follow-up." He waited a beat to let the hook firmly grab hold. "We're living rich."

He's right. When you truly work for yourself you're living rich. By figuring out what your own real work needs are, and by working to achieve them, you'll finally start to feel good about yourself. You'll feel a new and unique sense of freedom and personal empowerment. In effect, you'll have used your earnings to buy the freedom to do whatever it is you want. Remember: To be free is to live rich, and to live rich is to be free.

When you're not truly working for yourself, you're a wage slave. I'm no Marxist, but when you're working for your boss, or even for your parents, rather than for yourself, you're enslaved. Granted, they may be chains of your own creation, consciously or unconsciously, but those are the strongest restraints.

A man can be kept in physical slavery by others, with shackles binding him, but if his will is unbroken he remains free in spirit. On the other hand, a man who chains himself to working for others feels no such sense of personal freedom. He may be physically free, but his spirit is in chains. He lives a poor life, regardless of how much money he is earning through his servitude. But if he breaks those psychological chains he is free to soar as high as his dreams will take him. With neither physical nor psychological restraints holding him back, he can finally live rich. All that's standing between you and such a flight to freedom is your current relationship to money and work.

Make Money

Money is a crucial ingredient for living a rich life. And work is the way we make money. It's ironic, but by accepting those two apparently materialistic concepts you can achieve spiritual and emotional freedom. By entering into, and mastering, the worlds of money and work, you can transcend them. But to do that you need to set aside some of the attitudes and beliefs you've absorbed in the past.

THE STORY OF LEIF HEIDSICK

I've known Leif Heidsick since he was ten years old. He was a childhood friend of my son's. They met on Martha's Vineyard where both families vacationed. Each summer, between the ages of ten and sixteen, my son and Leif were inseparable. Leif's father was, at one time, deputy mayor of the city of New York. A dedicated servant of the people, he became dean of an alternative university when he left City Hall. Leif was taught the importance of service. He learned the lesson well.

After graduating from an elite private college in New England with a philosophy degree, Leif went on to get a master's degree in psychology from an Ivy League university and then a doctorate from a divinity school. He was ordained as a minister and eventually was named "minister for social action" at one of New York City's largest and most liberal Protestant congregations. During his years at college Leif had met, and married, Trudi.

They make a fascinating couple. Leif is tall and strikingly hand-some, with deep-set eyes and a full beard. Look up "wholesome" in the dictionary and you'll find a picture of Trudi. Her midwestern good looks dramatically play off Leif's prophetic appearance. It's as if John the Baptist married Laura Ingalls.

When they first moved to New York, Trudi found a job as an assis-tant producer at a local television station. She immediately took the New York media by storm and moved from one plum assignment to another.

Meanwhile, Leif was finding there was more to social action than he'd thought. He had been prepared to deal with governmental bureau-cracy and even perhaps some reticence from the congregation. What he wasn't prepared for was the politics of the church. He had been willing to forgo the kind of salary his expensive education could otherwise command to help others. But he wasn't sure he was willing to sacrifice his family's financial future to stay in just another power-obsessed bureaucracy.

He first came to see me as a client, not a friend, after eight years at the church. He and Trudi were expecting their second child and he wanted to go over their financial situation. After about thirty minutes it was clear to me that Trudi was happy at her work and that they were both happy in their Manhattan apartment. The problem was Leif. He was miserable at work. Being raised to give service, and being a member of the clergy, he was loath to admit the problem, however. Finally I said, "Leif, I've known you since you were ten years old. There's no reason to be embarrassed with me. There's nothing wrong with you. You just want to make money."

MONEY: MANKIND'S GREATEST INVENTION

Money doesn't get the credit it deserves. I believe it's mankind's great-est invention because it can buy you almost anything.

We've always been taught that money can't buy happiness. But let's examine that statement for a second. It's true that money cannot directly buy happiness . . . but can't it buy things that make you happy? Think about the things that make *you* happy. I'll bet most of them can be purchased, in one form or another. Obviously the happi-ness that comes from physical experiences can be purchased, but so too can many emotional and psychological experiences. The joy of listening to music, of seeing art, of reading a book, can all be bought with money. And while having money may not automatically make you happy, not having money can certainly make you unhappy. In fact, studies repeatedly show that financial problems are the most common cause of unhappiness.

I think psychologist Herb Goldberg, coauthor (along with Robert T. Lewis) of the classic book *Money Madness: The Psychology of Saving, Spending, Loving, and Hating Money*, summed up this issue very well. "Happiness," he wrote, "generally comes as a by-product of some other experience or the achievement of some other goal, not as an end in itself; so it cannot be bought with money, but money may well increase your range of experiences or your opportunities to achieve goals, which, in turn, bring about happiness."

Another great shibboleth of those who denigrate money is that it can't buy health. Really? What world have they been living in? Certainly not the one where the cost, efficiency, and effectiveness of health care are the subjects of our nation's great debates. Money can buy you the finest doctors and the greatest medical care in the world. It can sometimes buy previously infertile couples the ability to have children. It can also buy you the most effective pharmaceuticals available. Prozac and Viagra aren't being given away, you know.

And it's not just treatment where money can make a big difference; money helps with prevention as well. Money can buy you the advice and tutelage of a dietitian and nutritionist. It can buy you the motivation and knowledge of a personal trainer. At the very least money can buy you exercise equipment, a health club membership, dietary supplements, vitamins, and lots of fat-free snacks. I know, you can buy healthy foods for very little money. However, it's a lot more convenient to eat those expensive low-fat prepared foods than it is to make your own rice and beans from scratch. And convenience, for better or worse, is what dictates whether most people do something or don't. Simply put, studies have shown that people in higher income brackets tend to be healthier.

Okay, money cannot buy you a new set of genes . . . yet. If (I should probably say when) the technology becomes available to alter genetic factors that contribute to disease, do you think it's going to be expensive and available only to those with the most money, or do you think the average bean-counting HMO is going to be quick to foot the bill?

Can money buy love? Well, I'll admit money can't buy you the spiritual love of another human being. However, it *can* buy you physical love. In fact, that was probably one of its earliest uses. After all, prostitution is called the world's "oldest profession." Money can even buy a form of spiritual love, albeit not from another human. Anyone who has ever bought a dog knows that, on some level, he's buying unconditional love. And certainly money can buy companionship. Go to any area where there are lots of senior citizens and you're apt to find some homely, boring, but affluent fellow who's going out every night of the week with a different lovely and interesting woman.

Money truly comes into its own when you're dealing with material purchases. It's money that allows the lawyer and the farmer and the shoemaker and the shepherd all to interact in the marketplace. Before the invention of money, people could get things only by bartering. As a lawyer, if I wanted to get food from the farmer all I had to trade for it was my legal skill. Unless he was involved in a property dispute with one of his neighbors, my family would go hungry. My kids would do without shoes until the shoemaker got sued by someone. And we'd have no wool for clothing until the shepherd decided to draft his will. Without money society would have remained in small bands of nomadic hunter/gatherer and compact agrarian villages.

The magic of money is in its plasticity. It has a protean quality, the ability to become whatever you want it to be. Having no value of its own, it becomes the most valuable substance of all, since it can be turned into anything and everything. But it's this very adaptability that has also made it a taboo subject.

MONEY: THE ULTIMATE TABOO

Admit it: My effusive praise of money has made you a bit uncomfortable. Perhaps it has made you think less of me. And maybe, if some of my logic struck home, you felt guilty about it. Somehow, money isn't supposed to be looked on with such awe and even reverence.

First let me set something straight. I'm not worshiping money. I don't love money more than I love my family, my friends, or even my pets. But I don't hate money either. I look at it in as neutral a manner as I possibly can. I see it as a remarkable tool to get whatever I need and want. And since it can enable you and me to live rich, it's something deserving of respect. Such a neutral view of money isn't common. And because it's so rare, it's often confused with greed. Greed is wanting money for its own sake. I want money for what it can do for me. I think that's being rational, not greedy.

Second, let me point out that most of those who say there's something wrong with money don't have much of it. You don't hear the wealthy bad-mouthing money. That's because it's natural for people to view their own traits in a positive light. While in most cases this is a healthy defense mechanism, when it comes to money it can be disastrous.

Americans weren't always so hung up about money. In the eighteenth and nineteenth centuries Americans were very hung up about sexuality. The Puritans were . . . puritanical. The Victorians were repressed. Yet during those times, the pursuit of money was seen as a positive thing. Wealth was praiseworthy. Today we're the opposite. Sex and sexual openness are considered healthy and valuable. Rather than progressing psychologically, I think America has just traded one set of hang-ups for another.

Setting aside debates on morality, getting sex out of the closet seems to have helped individuals. Many of the medical problems that were historically associated with sexual hysteria and repression have eased. But at the same time, medical problems associated with money attitudes—such as low self-confidence, low self-esteem, and feelings of low social competence—have increased. I think it's time for money to come out of the closet.

Most of my clients have a very hard time viewing money rationally. That's because of its very nature. Because it is the proverbial tabula rasa it has become the ultimate talisman or fetish—an object invested with supernatural power that can transform us and our surroundings. Money is a blank slate on which you can project all your psychological, emotional, and spiritual problems.

That's how the Freudians came up with their infamous equation that money equaled feces. They believe the first medium on which we project our psyche is our own feces. During toilet training, they say, we learn that we can please our parents by either releasing or withholding our feces. As we grow up, we withhold (save) or release (spend) money in the same manner as we did our feces. Now, in general, I'm neither pro- nor anti-Freudian. However, in this case I think they're clearly taking things a little bit too far. Perhaps the obsessive hoarder and the compulsive spender are working out their toilet train-

ing through their money. But I don't believe we all are. Besides, if
money was truly as dirty as Freudian psychoanalysts claim, would they
charge so much for their services?

I'll admit that was a low blow. But there's a deeper truth underlying it. Analysts and therapists of every school have a terrible time
dealing with money. That's because their relationship with patients or
clients is financial as well as therapeutic. There's no getting around
the fact that clients pay therapists for their time. As a result, money is
an issue therapists can't readily discuss. So while all manner of sexual
deviation and obsession is fair game in a therapy session, money issues
generally remain buried. Today money, not sex, is the ultimate taboo.

Analysts, when surveyed about what they should never do with
patients, felt that lending money to patients was far worse than hit-
ting them or even having sex with them. The Jungian analyst James
Hillman has joked that patients more readily reveal what's concealed
by their pants than what's hidden in their pants' pockets.

Projecting our psyches onto money is doubly problematic. Not only
do you have no one to discuss this with—since therapists steer clear of
the issue—but you're projecting onto something that's central to your
ability to survive and thrive in the world; central, I believe, to your
being able to live rich. It's one thing to project your problems onto,
say, high-heeled shoes. It's quite another to project them onto the tool
you need to provide all your physical and most of your emotional
needs, the tool that will enable you to live rich.

WHY A "LITTLE BIT MORE" CAN NEVER BE ENOUGH

I want to take a moment's break at this point to resolve a dilemma
that plagues almost every client who comes to see me. Have you often
felt that just "a little bit more money" was all you needed? Didn't it
seem that you were just a few dollars short of getting everything you
wanted? Then, when you actually got those few dollars, what happened? You stayed just a few dollars short of achieving your goals.
Why? A number of things contribute to your always feeling like
you're just short of your goals.

First, there's inflation. By the time you actually get those added
dollars they're worth less than they were when you dreamed of them,
and all the things you dreamed of buying have simultaneously gone
up in price.

Second, there's a failure to realize that dreams always expand beyond your wallet. Henry Clay Lindgren, the author of the excellent book *Great Expectations: The Psychology of Money*, noted that "in a threatening and unstable world we could always use more of the things that money can provide, whether security or more power or whatever; the need for a little bit more is universal and eternal."

And third, just as dreams expand beyond your wallet, so spending expands to at least equal available funds. Remember: Money has no value of its own. When most of us get a raise or receive a windfall, we don't feel that it's real until it's spent. Sitting in an account somewhere, those added dollars are too abstract to bring us any joy. But spend them on something we've coveted and they're very real. Of course, they're also gone.

The solution is to accept that the problem isn't really the exact amount of dollars you have, or even the size of your dreams; it's your attitude toward money and work. When you're truly working for yourself, when you're working to fulfill your own real needs, you won't need a few more dollars to finally get to where you want to be . . . you'll be there already.

MONEY: THE ROOT OF ALL CONFUSION

Not only is money the ultimate taboo, but it's also considered by many to be evil. Much of this belief comes from mistaken notions about what religions teach about money. The most common misconception is citing the Bible as saying, "Money is the root of all evil." The actual quotation is "The love of money is the root of all evil." I agree with that. I believe you should use money to buy the things you love. I don't think you should love money itself. It's the world's most powerful tool, but it's still just a tool. I don't love my laptop computer or CD player either.

Throughout history, religions, particularly Christianity, have had complex relationships with money. I've already paraphrased Christ's admonition to render unto Caesar the things that are Caesar's and unto God the things that are God's. That, however, could be balanced by quoting that it's easier for a camel to pass through the eye of a needle than for a rich man to enter the kingdom of heaven. This mixed message is mirrored by the preaching of the virtue of poverty from bejeweled pulpits in opulent churches.

As a society we have incorporated this mixed message and ambiguity into our own attitudes toward money. We believe that "you get what you pay for," yet we fall for all sorts of cons thinking we can "get something for nothing." We think coveting money is crass and in poor taste, yet we make celebrities out of the very wealthy. We say people's value is based on who they are, not how much money they have, yet we clearly defer to the wealthy.

The Jungian Adolf Guggenbühl-Craig believes religions have problems with money for the same reasons they often have problems with sexuality. Both sexuality and money are projection carriers for the psyche. Most religions, on the other hand, ask you to project your psyche, or soul, onto them instead. Christianity, for instance, says you can achieve salvation only through Jesus Christ. That means the worldly projections of your psyche—sex and money—are the competitors of religion in a battle of good and evil.

I have my own theory, and while I'm not a trained analyst or a theologian, I do have some practical experience working with people and their money. I think the problem lies in the misguided and outdated rules and beliefs about money that my clients have been taught. I think they're conflicted about money because on some level they know the things they've been taught about it—particularly how it relates to work—just don't make any sense

The Protestant ethic that infuses American culture isn't anti-money. In fact, it says wealth is a sign of God's favor. But it also says affluence should come as a result of hard work. Now we all know you can sometimes make a good living by working hard. But we also know that no one, other than a movie star or a professional athlete, ever becomes rich through a salary for hard work. Affluence and wealth almost always come from inheritance, speculation, or risk taking (unearned income), not from hard work (earned income). And many times great fortunes are based on somewhat elastic ethics. (They were called robber barons for a reason.) There's an old saying that behind every great fortune there's a great crime.

My clients have been told they should value everyone's contribution to society. Yet society clearly values some people more than others: The lawyer and the gardener are not given equal status. And those who are valued the highest aren't always those who are most important to society. Teachers are paid very low wages compared with lawyers. Yet which profession is more important to society?

My clients have been taught that their value as human beings has nothing to do with their salaries. And yet if they're offered less than they expected as a salary or in payment for their services they take it as a personal affront to their worth as a human being. They say they think it's what inside that counts and yet they—and everyone else—respond, positively or negatively, to how people look. Someone who's dressed in expensive clothes, driving an expensive car, gets treated better than someone who isn't.

My clients have been led to believe that pay should somehow equate with the work performed. And yet they can see that's not the case. Older workers have historically gotten more money than younger workers, not because they produced more, but because they had seniority. Managers have been paid more than workers, not because they do any more, or work any harder, but because they have more status.

My clients have been told that anyone can become rich, yet they see the rich get richer and the poor get poorer. They've been taught the rags-to-riches myth and, like the rest of us, love the occasional real-life example of it, but all the while they know that it takes money to make money and that often it's who you know, not what you know, that counts.

Perhaps most damaging of all, my clients have been taught they should pay more attention to the emotional and psychological elements of work than to the money. The money, they were told, would take care of itself. They'd automatically be rewarded for their hard work. They thought that if they did what they loved, the money would follow. Their pay would magically match their education, their emotional gratification, and their perception of their own worth. They were told to ignore money. In this case ignorance clearly was not bliss.

PAY AND PERFORMANCE AREN'T RELATED

It's obvious that any automatic system of rewards for hard work, education, or personal worth is a thing of the past.

The industrial age's employer/employee unwritten contract has been shredded. No longer can you assume that doing your job satisfactorily will guarantee continued employment. Today you could be let go from your job as a personnel manager for Ishmael's Coffee Inc. because a drought in Guatemala cut into the supply of beans for the company's popular Latin Hi Test blend.

No longer can you assume doing your job well will guarantee a raise or a promotion. A pat on the back isn't even certain. A kick out the door is just as likely. Your hard work could be rewarded with the elimination of benefits, a pay cut, the termination of your support staff, or perhaps even a layoff.

Today your performance has little or no effect on your long-term job security. You are just part of a long list of expense items that can be trimmed, cut, sliced, or diced in response to any outside stimuli. If the CEO wants to boost the value of his golden parachute of stock options, he can decide to cut your entire division. As a result, Wall Street applauds, his benefits package goes up $500,000 in value, and you're out of work through no fault of your own.

Actually, I don't believe there was ever really any direct correlation between your performance and your long-term job security . . . unless of course you were employed on a piecework basis. Compensation in the workplace has never been related to performance. Instead it has always been based on organizational status and supply and demand.

In hierarchical organizations, such as large institutions or corporations, pay has always been automatic, but tied to how high up you were on the ladder. Performance and productivity meant little. What counted was how many people were under you.

Let's say you were one of a handful of clerks in Acme Inc.'s shipping department. The longer you stayed with the company, the more pay increases you got (based on length of service, not performance). That meant that the most senior clerk was the highest paid. If you were lucky enough to be senior clerk when the foreman either retired, moved up the ladder, was fired, or died, you might become the new foreman. That resulted in an increase in pay, probably of about 30 to 40 percent, not because you were suddenly working any harder or any better, but because you now had a level of personnel beneath you.

The more levels you could climb above, the higher your salary would rise. This formula wasn't a complete secret. There were a few canny individuals who figured out this equation. You could spot them because they were the ones always suggesting ways of adding yet another layer of management.

In the professions, supply and demand has been the primary determinant of pay. This has historically been accomplished by establishing craft guilds and apprenticeship systems. This effectively limits the number of individuals who would perform the task. If they banded together and made sure there were only one hundred plumbers in the state at any one time, each of those lucky one hundred was pretty much guaranteed a good living. White-collar professionals do the same thing, except by severely limiting the number of people who enter exclusive training programs. If you limit the number of law schools and their size, and make it difficult and expensive to enter the school and pass the bar exam, you keep the number of lawyers down and make sure each of you makes a good living.

Even with all the evidence to the contrary, lots of my clients believed that they would be rewarded for their hard work with increased pay. Why? Because that's what they were told, over and over. Management practiced the Big Lie, believing if they said this nonsense long enough and often enough people would buy it and work harder as a result. Bosses at every level said, "If you do your job well you'll get rewarded." And yet every raise request was turned into a reward not for performance, but for length of service or for climbing the ladder. Despite everything they could see with their own eyes—the incompetence above them, the injustice of office politics, individuals raised to their highest level of incompetency—my clients kept plugging away. Those who had a sense of what was really happening joined a profession, started clawing their way up the ladder, or launched their own business. And those who were still in the dark when the layoffs of the past two decades began were soon jolted awake by the sound of all those desks around them being emptied.

According to the *New York Times* 1996 special report, *The Downsizing of America*, three fourths of all American households had a "close encounter" with a layoff from 1980 through 1996. One third of all households in the study reported that a family member had lost a job. An additional 40 percent said they knew a relative, friend, or neighbor who was laid off. The study reported that one out of every ten adults (that's 19 million people) acknowledged a recent lost job in their household has led to a major crisis.

By now, anyone who's sentient realizes there's no such thing as justice in the workplace. But remarkably, most people, particularly my baby boomer clients, are still buying into a similar myth: that the emotional and psychological rewards of work are just as important as, if not more important than, its monetary rewards.

DO IT FOR THE MONEY AND THE LOVE WILL FOLLOW

Clearly, for some people, this preference for meaning over money comes from the previously mentioned neurotic belief that money is dirty. But for most of my clients, who by and large are baby boomers, the reasons run far deeper, mirroring the depth of their drive for self-actualization.

(Someone who talks or writes about a large group of people, such as the baby boom generation, has to engage in some sweeping generalizations. I'm as guilty of this as anyone. Clearly there are baby boomers who don't fit the mold . . . and some of them will be reading this book. To those readers I can only apologize. I'm sorry for overlooking your uniqueness. However, I have to remind you that, even though you may not share all your cogenerationalists' traits, you are nevertheless impacted by those traits and society's responses to them.)

The baby boom is the largest and most studied generation in history. Simply because of their numbers, the 76 million boomers have had an enormous impact on society. Their concerns and obsessions have become America's concerns and obsessions. When they were infants, America was one big Romper Room. When they were teens, America was Pepperland. When they were in their acquisitive twenties and thirties America was The Sharper Image. When they began to start having families America became Toys R Us. Now as they're entering middle age, America is Club Nautilus, where those paunches and sags can be firmed up. And when they grow old, America will be one big Del Boca Vista senior community.

In addition, as the generation born after World War II, at a time when there seemed to be no limits to what America could do, they were heralded as the golden children of the future. They were so important that moms stayed home to take care of them and suburbs were built for their care and comfort. Dr. Spock said they should be coaxed rather than forced, and their schedules should be flexible rather than fixed. Instead of being taught the basics in schools, boomers were taught to think critically. These golden kids wouldn't fall for commie propaganda, they'd be individualists and idealists. And so they are.

All of these facts led boomers to grow up with a sense of their own destiny and an extraordinary self-awareness. Some say this is why boomers are arguably the most self-absorbed generation in history. They believed, and some continue to believe, that their generation had a special mission. They were going to build the perfect country.

But their sheer size got the better of them. As they got older they wanted the best of everything, just like when they were kids. But unfortunately, there were too many of them. Real estate prices soared while wages, in real terms, remained stagnant. To even briefly approximate the lifestyles of their parents both boomer spouses had to work. And even that hasn't been enough. Arguably the real world inhabited by boomers has gotten worse, not better. Divorce, illegitimacy, crime, suicides, drug and alcohol problems, and almost every other social ill has gotten worse during the adult lives of boomers.

Their parents' generation measured success objectively: house in the suburbs, big car with lots of chrome, lots of well-dressed kids with Mom staying home to care for them all. Boomers just can't measure up to their parents in that manner. So what was the golden generation to do? Change the measuring stick, of course. Instead of measuring success objectively, they would measure it subjectively. Since boomers couldn't perfect the exterior world, they would perfect themselves. They'd eat better than their parents and work out. They'd say it was emotional, spiritual, and psychological success that counted. Their consciousness was higher than that of their parents, and so that made them better. Some, in fact, would say they were choosing this path, whether that meant living on a commune in the 1970s or pursuing "voluntary simplicity" in the 1990s. Most of all, they wouldn't lead "divided" lives like their parents.

The parents of the baby boom (and truth be told, every generation other than the baby boom) compartmentalized their lives. There was work and there was life. They did the former to enjoy the latter. During the workweek they'd labor away, putting in their time, doing what society wanted of them. Then, on the weekend, they'd retreat into their private suburban Edens and do what *they* wanted. When in college, boomers saw this as a terrible compromise. College students always decry this kind of arrangement. They dismiss the "worker ants" and say *they'll* pursue fields that offer self-discovery and contribute to society. That's easy to say while you are in college and your basic needs are being addressed. All most students have to do is pass their exams. Once most people get out into the real world and suddenly have bills to pay, they compromise and compartmentalize their lives. Boomers, however, haven't; they've remained perpetual students.

Boomers generally don't see a split between their private and public worlds. They don't want to put their pockets before their principles five out of seven days a week. They believe they should be able to get both financial and personal fulfillment on the job. They think it's actually unhealthy to split your life into two. Instead they want a synthesized life, one in which they spend seven days a week doing fulfilling things. Some boomers even think their employer or business owes them emotional as well as financial compensation. They think they have an inalienable right to meaningful work. For a little while, at least, they were able to express this right.

Boomers were able to hold on to this student attitude because their basic needs were still being addressed even after they got out of college. The economy was doing well, creating lots of jobs. Sure, wages were stagnant in real terms, but with both spouses working they could afford to at least superficially maintain the trappings of their parents' lives. Boomers who were skilled or educated were almost always able to get jobs that matched their skill or training. Society was taking care of the boomers, just as their parents did. But then the bubble burst.

During the recession of the late 1980s society pulled the rug out from under the boomers' Nike-clad feet. Suddenly, with the economy shifting from an industrial to an information basis, and from a domestic to global marketplace, the nation couldn't afford to prop up the lifestyle of the baby boom generation. Employers started cutting all those layers of management in an effort to remain competitive. Fulfillment? Hell, employers aren't even guaranteeing health insurance coverage anymore.

Remember learning about Maslow's hierarchy of needs back in Psych 101? Well, let me refresh your memory: Abraham Maslow ranked human needs, saying that as each in turn was satisfied, people would concentrate on the next. He said the most fundamental needs were physiological—basically food, clothing, and shelter. Second were safety needs—things that ensured you weren't in physical danger. Third came the needs to feel that you belong to a group and are loved. Fourth, he believed, was the need for esteem. Finally, the fifth and highest need, the one people concentrate on when all other needs are met, is self-actualization.

Most boomers are still acting as if all their other needs were being met on the job and all they had to concentrate on was self-actualization. That's crazy. Jobs and businesses are so tenuous today that concentrating on anything other than the first two needs is a stretch for most of us. It's self-defeating to search for self-actualization when you should be worrying about keeping a roof over your head. You're not going to end up being self-actualized sleeping in a cardboard box out in the rain.

I think it was noble for baby boomers to try to lead a rich life seven days a week. But in the process they are actually leading a much poorer life than their parents. In their efforts to make sure their work life has meaning, they shortchange their home lives. They spend less time doing the very things where meaning and fulfillment are easier to come by: taking their dog for a walk, sitting under a tree with their family, reading a good book, praying to God.

I tell my clients it's a mistake to *look* for meaningful work. If you can *find* it, that's great. It's wonderful to be able to get both emotional and financial satisfaction from a job or business. But to set out to look for it, and to make that your goal in the workplace, is almost certain to lead to frustration, if not outright misery. Not only won't you live rich, you'll live miserable. To live rich you need to abandon the pursuit of meaningful work. You can keep the attainment of it as a dream, but don't count on it. Look to your work to satisfy your physiological and safety needs by providing you with money. Look to the rest of your life to satisfy your needs for belongingness, love, esteem, and self-actualization. To the extent you can maximize the amount of money you earn through work you'll increase your chances of satisfying those other needs outside of work. Isn't that the more sensible approach?

I think people have a mistaken impression of the now-popular credo: "Do what you love, the money will follow."* Some people seem to think this means that the secret to making money is to do something you love. I simply don't think that's true. As evidence, just look at the thousands of struggling and impoverished actors, writers, sculptors, and painters who are forced to work as waiters in New York City. And I know this isn't isolated to the Big Apple. As I understand it, the actual argument is that by doing something you love rather than something you don't, your need for money will be lessened. Perhaps the philosophy would be better expressed as "Do what you love and

---

*I certainly don't blame Marsha Sinetar, author of the best-selling book with that title, for this mistaken impression. I think many people hear the title and read into it what they want—without actually reading the book itself. Having written a book called *Die Broke,* I have firsthand knowledge of this phenomenon.

you'll be happy with whatever money follows." I must admit that I take a far more material view of things. I don't believe people's need for money automatically decreases or increases because of what they're doing. Their wants may well change . . . but not their needs.

As I've said before, work isn't meant to provide fulfillment; it's meant to provide money. By asking it to provide more you're working against its nature. You don't ask the rest of your life to provide you with money, do you? You don't go to your children and ask them to put food on your table. You don't go to your house of worship and ask it to maintain the roof over your head. You don't expect the book you're reading to serve as a garment as well. Work is for money, the rest of life is for everything else. Accept that principle and you'll be able to live rich. So you won't be able to spend seven days a week, twenty-four hours a day doing what you want. But you will finally be able to spend your time off work doing exactly what you want. Living rich is a question of quality, not quantity.

THE SECRETS OF MAKING MONEY

How do you apply a new, more rational attitude toward money? Well, the second half of this book offers my very targeted pragmatic advice about doing just that. For now, however, let me offer some more general suggestions. I'll be coming back to these ideas throughout the rest of the book, so don't feel as though you've got to memorize them all right now.

Make Money a Priority

Perhaps the single most important secret about how to make money is the simplest: Make it a priority. Those who earn a great deal of money do so because they spend a lot of time thinking about how to make money and a lot of energy doing the things that make them money. They consciously stress the importance of money in all their work and business actions. I tell my clients to regularly ask themselves why they are doing their work, and to answer: "To make money."

Focus on the Future

To make money you really need to be able to make successful "investments" in yourself as well as the stock market. And just as having some idea of what will happen in the future can help your stock

investments, so too will a future orientation help your personal investments. Become a student of your company, profession, and industry.
Watch trends in your state, county, and town. Try to discern what's
likely to happen before it becomes obvious.

You don't need to be a seer. Most people are so lost in the minutiae
of their individual lives that they fail to look around them. They won't
know their company is faring poorly until a pink slip lands on their
desk. And it's only when they discover no other company is hiring
that they'll figure out the industry as a whole is going downhill. To
live rich you need to learn to spot future trends in your department,
your company, your industry, your profession, your market, your town,
and your region, and act on them.

Pick Your Parents

Studies have shown that the children of successful people often
become successful themselves. In effect, they learn by watching. But
that doesn't mean you're doomed to follow in your parents' economic
footsteps: You just need to find another set of parents. In all seriousness, if your parents didn't teach you how to make money, find mentors who will. In my own case, I learned about the importance of
focusing on making money from my first law partner, Manny Zimmer.
I learned how to collect accounts receivable from a friend, Kenny Tillman, who is a very successful retailer. In retrospect, I also learned
about long-term financial planning from my father-in-law, who used
to drive me crazy.

Bust Your Butt

Making money is hard work. You have to wake up earlier, work
harder all day long, and go to sleep later than everyone else. The only
ways to make money without hard work are to inherit it and to win
the lottery.

Put Yourself in the Right Place

Hard work will only get you so far. To make money you also need to
be in the right place at the right time, and to know the right people.
That doesn't just mean attending the "right" school and belonging to
the "right" clubs, though that doesn't hurt at all. It also means becoming an active and involved person in whatever you do, and letting peo-

ple know you're accessible and available. Join professional and trade associations and mingle at group functions. Become part of a religious congregation and attend services. Help out with the PTA at your child's school. Talk to people at your health club. Get involved in local politics. You guarantee you'll be at the right place at the right time by being in the right places *all* the time.

Stop Blaming Others

Feeling like a powerless victim, as I'll explain in Chapter 4, is one of the most difficult hurdles to overcome if you want to live rich. To make money you'll have to get over the idea that you're somehow a victim. That's because blaming others keeps you from taking charge of your life. In the game of life, you cannot reap large rewards without taking charge.

Don't Compare Yourself to Others

Every moment you spend working to keep others down or worrying about someone else's success, is a moment you could better have spent making money for yourself. Living rich is not a zero sum game. There isn't a limited amount of riches out there. Someone else's success doesn't diminish you. And someone else's failure doesn't improve your life one bit.

Don't Get Angry, Succeed

Anger is an impotent emotion. All it does is get in your way and inhibit thoughtful action. Believe me, I get just as angry as anyone else. But I try never to act on that anger. I do my best to base my actions on rational judgments. I vent my feelings, count to ten, walk around the block, or do whatever else it takes to blow off steam. Then, and only then, do I decide what to do. Your success is the best possible revenge for any wrong. And the best way to be successful is to think before you act.

Don't Feel Content Unless You Are

Contentment is a wonderful emotion . . . if it's justified. When you're content you're no longer motivated to change things. And making money requires motivation and being dissatisfied with the status quo I tell my clients to make sure their contentment is real and not just their way of rationalizing not making the effort to change things. If you're truly content, then you're already living rich.

Don't Be Overly Sentimental

There's nothing wrong with being sentimental toward family and friends. But when it comes to business and the workplace, excessive sentiment can get in the way of making money. If you let emotions enter into what would otherwise be rational financial decisions you're making it harder to make money. Just as you should look to your life rather than your work for self-actualization, so too should you reserve your sentiment for life rather than work. You can be as sentimental and emotional as you want . . . after business hours.

Change Your Self-Image

In many ways we're our own worst enemies. There are a lot of people who don't make money because they can't see themselves making money. Because the goal of a rich life seems so far removed from what they perceive to be their true self, they don't try all that hard to achieve it. It seems like a hopeless effort to them, so they don't give it 100 percent. Think of it this way. Have you ever been playing a game and fallen far behind? Did you try as hard as when the score was close, or did you start to coast, thinking why waste the energy and effort on a lost cause? If you see yourself as a loser you're not going to put the needed effort into making money, and you're never going to live rich. See yourself as a winner and you're more apt to become one.

LEIF HEIDSICK STARTS MAKING SOME MONEY

It took debate, self-analysis, and even some prayer before Leif came to me and admitted he was ready to start making money. Together we worked out a multipronged program for him to do just that.

First, he did everything he could to secure his political position in the church in order to provide a solid foundation.

Second, he updated his psychology education and got his New York State license so he could practice as a psychotherapist. I helped him open a small therapy practice while maintaining his job with the church. Through his contacts there, he quickly had more clients than he could handle.

Third, to broaden his market, I helped Leif promote himself through radio appearances and speeches.

Finally, after three years, it reached the point that his therapy practice began intruding on his duties at the church, and he made the leap of faith into business for himself.

Through it all he never gave up on social action. In fact, he's more active now than he was while at the church. Except today he's doing something rather than just preaching about doing something. His therapy practice and Trudi's media job are providing them with sufficient income that Leif can take off two weekends a month to lead peace and immigration rights marches on Washington along with some local activist groups. By making money he's finally doing what he wanted: He's helping people.

WHAT'S NEXT?

Shifting your attitude toward work and money, while the most dramatic part of the Live Rich program, is only the beginning. To finally live the life of your dreams you also need to alter the way you view career and business success. Rather than looking to climb a ladder or grow your business you've got to focus on change instead.

Don't Grow, Change   3

Established patterns can be very comforting. They can provide you with a sense of control over your increasingly complex and chaotic world. They can offer you a map to follow as you move through life. And they can give you a handy standardized gauge by which you can measure your progress.

Many of my clients, particularly the baby boomers who grew up in middle-class homes, had very comprehensive schedules laid out for them. By age seventeen they'd graduate high school. By the time they were twenty-two they'd have their bachelor's degree. When they hit twenty-five they'd get married. By thirty they'd have a house and a child, maybe with another on the way. In their forties they'd be sending their kids to college and paying for weddings. At fifty they'd be playing with grandchildren.

My clients started falling behind that mandated program right after college. In some cases it was because their generation's unique demographics made it economically impossible for them to stick to such an optimistic timetable. But for most of my clients, abandoning this conventional blueprint was a conscious act.

Coming of age in the 1960s and 1970s, they wanted to "do their own thing." Women and minorities saw their opportunities expand. Men realized there was more to life than growing up to become Ward Cleaver. As a result those personal game plans were altered or, in some cases, abandoned. Marriages were delayed, dismissed, or dissolved. Children were postponed . . . or ruled out altogether. Urban condos often replaced starter homes, and weekend cottages sometimes took the place of suburban split-levels.

I believe generations from now, sociologists will say that one of the great accomplishments of baby boomers was their destruction of these strict personal outlines and schedules.

Don't get me wrong: I think there's a place for order in the world. And I'm a firm believer in the right of society to make rules and restrict behaviors that could be harmful. I am, after all, a lawyer. But I think by letting someone else (whether it's a parent or priest) or something else (whether school system or social caste) tell you how to proceed through life and dictate what actions you should take, you give up your most precious possession, the one thing that enables you to live rich. your freedom to select your own destiny. By allowing yourself to be pushed along a predetermined path you're forced toward a goal that may not reflect your own needs. Those prescribed templates couldn't fit the individual needs of every man or woman. Being forced into a mold and pushed toward a goal that doesn't fit you can lead only to frustration and depression. Breaking free of these constraints and pressures emancipates your soul.

My only complaint about such a rebellion is that it hasn't gone far enough. Having freed themselves of the enforced ideas and expectations that cramped their personal lives, my clients failed to do the same with the chains that bound up their work and business lives.

THE STORY OF DEBBIE COOPER

Debbie Cooper and her husband, Ernie, first came to see me for a real estate consultation. My assistant Anthony had a hard time scheduling an appointment with the two of them, because of their schedules. I ended up telling Anthony to set up the meeting for a Saturday afternoon. My associate Jane Morrow and I were both a bit annoyed by this. But when it comes to the personal consulting business, the client's needs come first.

That was a very hard attitude for me to maintain once I met Ernie. A short, dark, stocky, frenetic fellow, he had the annoying habit of saying aloud everything he was thinking—whether or not it was appropriate. Since the meeting was on the weekend, both Jane and I had dispensed with our usual suits. So had Ernie, but just after we'd all shaken hands he muttered aloud, "For the fees you charge you both could have dressed better." I felt terrible . . . but only until I realized this was just the first note in a nasty running commentary.

Debbie, on the other hand, was warm and funny. She was tall, thin, relaxed, and raven-haired. She and Ernie didn't look or act like they belonged together. In fact, as I soon learned, they didn't.

Ernie was a stockbroker with a major investment house. Debbie was vice president of marketing for a well-known women's sports-wear manufacturer. Combined they earned over $300,000. They didn't have children and apparently weren't planning on them. They had a lovely co-op apartment on Manhattan's Upper West Side. But they spent very little time there. Both seemed to work night and day. Their jobs were their lives. They woke up and left the apartment at the crack of dawn. Debbie went to the gym—she was an avid runner and had begun entering triathlons. Ernie went to the office to get the early numbers from overseas markets. If they had the time they met for a late dinner at a restaurant. They spent some summer week-ends at a house they rented in the Hamptons, but even at the beach they had their laptops and cell phones within reach. They both seemed to be living separate and, to be brutally honest, empty lives. They told me they wanted help in finding a weekend house in Con-necticut.

After less than an hour with Ernie I knew enough not to question why they needed another piece of real estate to not spend time in. Instead we went over their finances and their real estate needs and wants. Then we all agreed to meet again in another two weeks to begin planning our house-hunting strategy. Once they left, Jane turned to me and said, "I think we'll be handling their divorce before we find them a weekend house." As usual, she was right.

We actually ended up helping Debbie find her divorce lawyer. She then came to us for help in buying an apartment of her own, since they'd sold the co-op and split the proceeds. Debbie became somewhat of a regular client. I helped her negotiate a couple of raises and set up an investment plan. She really blossomed after the divorce and began getting more and more serious about her running.

Debbie came to me one day to discuss a business opportunity. She had found it very tough to eat healthy meals while working such long hours and exercising so frequently. Debbie had begun packaging her own low-fat, high-protein meals and bringing them to the health club to heat up in the microwave. Some of her fellow triathletes tried the meals, loved them, and asked her to make them similar packages. One evening the owner of the club came over to the table where Debbie and five other triathletes were eating the prepared meals. After hearing about them, seeing their popularity, and tasting them, she asked Debbie if she'd be interested in selling them at the club's cafe. That's why Debbie came to me.

Debbie had found she loved coming up with the meals. She was also an extraordinary marketer—after all, that was her profession. But with the meals she'd be able to combine marketing with another of her loves—exercise. On the other hand, she was very happy with her job at the sportswear firm. She was established, respected, and earning over $150,000. "That was a lot to give up for a new business," she noted.

"Why do you have to give up your job?" I asked. "Why can't you do both?"

JOB, CAREER, AND BUSINESS PATTERNS

Americans approach their careers and businesses in a very linear fashion. Careers are climbs up hierarchical ladders. The archetypal tale is of someone starting off at the bottom rung in the corporation (it used to be the mailroom or secretarial pool—today it's as an administrative assistant) who eventually rises to be president. David Geffen, who actually did start off in the mailroom, is today's most oft-cited example of this climb up the ladder. The corresponding archetype for business is the little company, started by one or two people, that grows to become a multinational, multimillion-dollar corporation. For the past two decades Apple Computer has been the favorite example of this garage-to-boardroom tale. Both work patterns—the career as hierarchical climb and the business as ever-growing entity—are products of the industrial age.

The History of "Jobs"

Today the word "job" means a particular role in an organization—product manager for Apex Electronics' new Digicomp 800, for example. But that wasn't always the case. "Job" used to mean either a particular task—like shoveling out the stable—or a small amount of something—say, a load of lumber. Before the industrial age, "job" was a word that implied finite, short-term, and diverse. You did one job on Monday, and if you finished it, you did a different job on Tuesday. Or conversely, you unloaded the job of lumber from your wagon and then went to pick up another job, maybe of oats, to transport. You were doing whatever needed to be done on that particular day. Then along came Henry Ford.

Actually, even though I hate him, I can't blame it all on Henry Ford. He was just the most famous proponent of the move toward assembly line industrialization. Ford discovered that by standardizing activity he could produce more products, faster and more efficiently. Instead of mounting tires on Monday, and wiring headlights on Tuesday, depending on what needed to be done, a Ford assembly line worker did the same task every single day. The worker became a cog in the great wheel of industry. The age of the craftsman was ending.

The assembly line model wasn't applied just to manufacturing. All large businesses adopted it. Even if all a company did was push paper around from one desk to another, it turned its workplace into a factory floor and its workers into cogs in the machine, giving them each one specified task.

It is this standardization of work that changed the definition of "job" into today's usage. It's also responsible for alienating millions of people and killing millions of souls. Almost no one, other than the industrialists who made millions of dollars, likes this standardization of work. Before industrialization people took pride in their craft or profession. They enjoyed their work because it was challenging and varied. After industrialization work became a chore; a boring, deadening necessity. Thanks, Henry.

The History of Careers

With jobs now just steps in a process, the definition of career changed. Before industrialization people earned more by becoming better at what they did; perhaps your skill set you apart or maybe your efficiency led to greater personal profitability. In either case your compensation was linked to your performance. Your career consisted of an ongoing effort to improve your skill. With industrialization all this changed.

Mimicking the linear nature of the assembly line, industrial age organizations became more and more hierarchical. Companies were divided into divisions. Divisions were divided into departments. Departments were further divided into staff and management, perhaps with a manager, a deputy manager, a foreman, and a subforeman, overseeing the grunts. The company became a gigantic pyramid of individual jobs. The higher up the pyramid you were, the better your compensation—not because you did your job better, did more, worked harder, or generated more profit for the company, but simply because there were more people beneath you. To earn more money you needed to climb from one level up to the next.

Usually, the way to move up the pyramid was to put in your time. When the department manager moved up—perhaps because the division manager retired—the deputy manager moved up to manager, the foreman moved up to deputy manager, the subforeman moved up to foreman, and the senior grunt became subforeman. The same held true for nonindustrial businesses. Of course, if you were ambitious and were blocked by someone above you in the hierarchy who wouldn't or couldn't move, you could transfer into another department or look for a job higher up the pyramid in another company.

Careers became climbs up the hierarchy of organizations. Since time with the company was actually more important than proficiency or efficiency, moving from company to company was a detriment. If you changed employers often it was perceived as a sign of disloyalty, impatience, or lack of respect for the status quo. Of course, it could also have been seen as a sign of ambition, enthusiasm, and originality. However, none of those traits fit well with a hierarchical, bureaucratic mindset; they're too entrepreneurial.

The History of Business

Those who couldn't tolerate organizational politics could always go into business for themselves. As an entrepreneur running your own small company you could ignore hierarchy; you could get back to the kind of varied and rewarding work experience people had before industrialization turned them into worker bees. And as long as the company stayed small you could do it all and have it all: making money and enjoying work at the same time. But who wanted to stay small?

Small businesses were the norm in preindustrial America. The general store was a mom-and-pop operation. The blacksmith might have an apprentice, but that was all. The farmer had his family and perhaps a hired hand. Business owners worked very hard, but that work was directly translated into dollars for their wallets. Their concern was profitability—their personal bottom line—not their ego.

But in the industrial age things changed. To mass-produce you needed masses of staff and economies of scale. You couldn't run an assembly line with just two people. Big was good. The model for business success was the big corporation headed by the big baron of industry. It didn't matter what business you were in: Bigger was always better. Retailers aspired to be Sears Roebuck. Technology companies wanted to be Kodak. Manufacturers dreamed of becoming the next General Motors. Big meant an impressive location, a huge staff (with lots of hierarchical levels), and revenues in the millions.

Expansion was the only acceptable business plan in the industrial age. You might start with a single store, but as soon as you could beg, borrow, or steal the funds, you had to make that store bigger, open a second location, add to your product line, hire more staff. Rather than farming out tasks to other companies you had to bring them under your own roof. You needed a bookkeeper, a mail clerk, a marketing manager, and a human resources person. And once you had all those folks on board they each needed their own assistants. That was okay, since it meant getting bigger. What you used to be able to do yourself in an hour now took ten people and a week, but that was just the price of success.

Of course, as the company grew the reason it came into being faded into the background. The entrepreneur who couldn't stand bureaucracy and hierarchy was now atop a giant pyramid of his own making. The person who started a business to make money to satisfy his own needs was now working for the business's needs. The business was now a corporation, a truly separate entity with a life of its own. It was some kind of archetypal Frankenstein myth written in capitalist terms: The creation was no longer content to serve its creator's needs; it cared about its own needs. The profit finding its way into the owner's (or shareholders') pocket didn't matter as much as the size of the revenue stream feeding the corporate structure and enabling it to keep on growing.

INFORMATION TECHNOLOGY HAS CHANGED EVERYTHING

The job and business patterns of the industrial age have become out-dated thanks to the technological revolution that has ushered us into the information age. Information technology (primarily telecommunications and personal computers) has changed our personal lives in thousands of ways we know about, and probably thousands of others we haven't yet realized. The effects of new technology on work are just as sweeping and even more clear-cut.

Information technology has enabled business to be conducted faster than ever before. Decisions that used to require months of research and weeks of analysis can now be made in days. Work that previously took days can now be done in hours.

Information technology has allowed an individual to do work that used to require a department, a department to do the work that used to require a division, and a division to do the work of an entire company. An individual auto worker can now control ten robot welders. A single magazine editor can now do his own writing, photography, page layout, and typesetting.

Information technology has eliminated the need for support staff. A personal computer can now function as an administrative assistant, answering and placing telephone calls, sending and receiving faxes and e-mail, keeping track of appointments and correspondence. Software can now let an individual entrepreneur also serve as her own book-keeper, secretary, receptionist, art department, and public relations manager, among other things.

Information technology has led to a global marketplace. An engineering firm in Calcutta can provide services to an auto parts maker in Milwaukee just as efficiently as a competing engineering firm located in Chicago . . . and vice versa. That auto parts maker can ship its hubcaps to an auto maker in Rome just as quickly as a hubcap maker in Naples.

Information technology has enabled smaller firms to compete on an almost equal footing with larger firms. Just as Amazon.com was able to come from seemingly nowhere to compete with corporate book-sellers like Barnes & Noble and Borders, so too can a single person launch a specialty book business on the Internet and successfully compete with Amazon.com for business.

It's clear that information technology threatens the extinction of the large hierarchical organization. Sure, there are still going to be huge multinationals. IBM and Nestlé aren't folding up their three-piece suits and going home. But to survive and thrive, to be able to respond quickly to the constant changes in the marketplace, even the largest organization is becoming smaller, streamlining its bureaucracy, decentralizing decision making—in effect, becoming more like a small business. They're listening to, and following, Tom Peters's and Bob Waterman's famous advice to "stick to their knitting." They've focused on their "core competency," and in their "search for excellence" have reinvented themselves and turned the world of their employees upside down.

JOBS, CAREERS, AND SMALL BUSINESS IN THE INFORMATION AGE

The rush to downsize over the past decade has forever changed the American workplace. One third of all households have had a family member lose a job since 1980, according to the *New York Times* 1996 special report on downsizing. Obviously, all those people who were laid off have had their lives changed dramatically. Some haven't been able to get new jobs. Many have, but they're earning less money than they were before. According to the *New York Times* study, only about 35 percent of those "downsized" who have found another job have ended up with a salary equal to or higher than what they were making previously. Even those who were spared the ax are now working longer hours, for the same money, perhaps with fewer benefits, and certainly with lower morale. The *New York Times* study calls the effect of downsizing on survivors "insidious," and notes that it has eliminated motivation and risk taking.

Certainly everyone realizes the old implied contract between employer and employee has been torn to shreds. Ironically, the very thing that has made companies feel secure—trimming staff—has made workers feel insecure. There are no longer any guaranteed raises, not even cost-of-living increases. Seniority today may mean a pink slip rather than a gold watch. A kid just out of college might be able to do your job almost as well as you, for two thirds of the money you're getting. For that savings they'll deal with lower productivity. Sacrifices for the company don't earn loyalty. The aerospace engineer who opts to move his family down to Texas when his Long Island–based employer is gobbled up can be laid off before his kids can memorize their new telephone number. In the words of futurist Watts Wacker, you're either an owner or a temp. You need to continually prove your value to the company if you expect to have your contract renewed.

The pyramid has been replaced by the diamond as the business structure of choice. Now you're one of a large group of equals working at the middle level, being supported by only a small number of people (perhaps just a single receptionist in the lobby) and with only a small number of strategic decision makers on top. As a result, your job is no longer the strictly defined set of tasks and responsibilities it was in the industrial age. Instead of being locked in a grid square, with people above and below and other departments alongside, you're now floating in a pool. You're expected to swim from project to project, team to team. On some you're supposed to take the lead and coach the team; on others you're just one of the players.

As a result, the industrial age career ladder has been chopped into kindling. With no hierarchy to climb, careers can no longer be clearly defined paths along well-marked steppingstones. Now careers are journeys into the unknown, with descents as well as climbs, diversions and detours as well as straightaways. And perhaps most frustrating of all, there's no clear finish line. Sure, becoming president of the company is possible, but it's less likely than ever before. Today there's so much movement from company to company that the next president is more apt to come from outside the organization. In fact, you're probably more likely to become president of another company than of the one for which you're currently working.

Just as jobs and careers have been forever changed by our entry into the information age, so too have small businesses. The career ladder with its well-defined steps and clear goal is gone, and so is the pattern of establishing a business. The old business model involved carving out a niche in an existing market and then increasing your market share. In the process your company grew in size and scope. As you grew you brought functions in-house. To gain market share you expanded your reach into new geographic areas. Perhaps you even expanded your product line. Your staff and physical plant grew along with your business. Your goal was to move from small business to big business. Think about the irony of that for just a moment. Here you are pulling out all the stops to get bigger . . . while the big businesses are hacking away at themselves trying to become smaller.

FOCUS ON CHANGE RATHER THAN GROWTH

Regardless of who signs your paycheck, to live rich in the twenty-first century you'll need to focus on change rather than growth. If you're going to make the money you need to live rich you can't let yourself be detoured by psychic benefits like corner offices, impressive titles, larger facilities, or bigger staffs. All they will do is interfere with your ability to meet your own real needs.

The key to meeting your own needs (that's what being successful at work now means) in the twenty-first century is flexibility. Whether you're an employee or an entrepreneur you must be able to take advantage of opportunities as soon as they appear. That's because such opportunities don't last very long in the information age.

Everything moves more quickly now. Markets appear overnight and vanish just as quickly. For example, in January everyone in your town starts talking about the new "wrap" sandwiches being sold at the health food store. In February some savvy entrepreneur starts selling them wholesale to delis in the area. In March another entrepreneur opens a "wraperia" restaurant downtown. Then in April there's a new buzz. Wraps are passé. Faux frankfurters are in.

The same is true in the workplace. Just about the time wraps are getting hot in your town, the trade magazine in your industry runs a story about how one of the mid-sized companies in the business has doubled sales because of its Web site. The week after the story appears everyone in your company receives a memo from the president announcing a meeting to establish a Web planning group. At the meeting the call goes out for anyone in the marketing department with the skill to plan a Web site. Suddenly there's a company Webmaster. Six months later the same trade magazine runs another article on the Internet, this time saying Web sites are just expensive promo pieces and don't really lead to increased sales. The Webmaster job will soon be history.

Obviously, to make my point I'm exaggerating the speed with which opportunities appear and then disappear . . . but not by much. In the information age windows of opportunity will open and shut more quickly than ever before. To be in position to spot and seize such fleeting chances employees and entrepreneurs will have to be lean and quick. Rather than a battleship forging straight ahead regardless of the weather, you need to be a Jet Ski, flitting from place to place, riding the waves rather than trying to cut through them.

You'll need this nimbleness not only to seize fleeting chances, but to compete with all the other Jet Skis out there. If you're an employee, all the people who used to be considered your coworkers or peers have also been thrown into the pool. They're now competing with you for the best opportunities. Entrepreneurs have to contend with all their traditional competitors, all the folks who were downsized and have started their own businesses, and all the old battleship organizations trying to act like Jet Skis. The waters are crowded and turbulent, and that means you've got to learn the secrets of staying afloat.

THE SECRETS OF CHANGING RATHER THAN GROWING

How do you make sure you keep from going under? Well, you focus on change rather than growth. And how do you do that? Once again, the second part of this book offers specific advice, but here I'll offer you some general principles and guidelines.

Don't Be a Company Man

You can't allow yourself to be too closely identified with any one company ... even if you're the owner. Anyone—employee or entrepreneur—who becomes an icon of the company he works for seriously inhibits his marketability. Your behavior and attitudes should be based on your own personal culture, not that of an organization. Your needs, not the company's, must be your priority. That doesn't mean you and the company are working at cross-purposes. If your needs and the company's needs aren't complementary, then it's time to change jobs or start a new business.

Don't Put Down Roots

Roots no longer secure you; they just slow you down. If you're an employee, treat your office like a hotel room, not your home away from home. All your personal needs and items should be able to fit in your briefcase and go home with you at night. There's nothing wrong with becoming friendly with coworkers, but don't let them dominate your social life. If the office is too cozy and all your friends are at the company, you'll hesitate when faced with a chance to leave. And if you don't seize an opportunity right away, it will be gone forever. This is a problem I see over and over again with my clients who have been employees of a particular company for more than three years.

If you're an entrepreneur no roots means renting rather than own-ing your location . . . unless it's also your home. In fact, don't buy any-thing you can rent or lease, whether it's a photocopier, a computer, a car, or a bookkeeper. Don't sink money into anything that's specific to one particular business or industry. Want to buy ten years' worth of letterhead to get the cheapest rate? Then make sure your logo and company name are generic enough to apply to any business in which you might find yourself.

Does the lack of roots make the workplace a less comfortable, less emotionally satisfying place? Perhaps, but I don't look at it that way. Instead I just think it makes the workplace more the way it should be: a place of business. I think there's actually danger in having a homey workplace. The more comfortable your workplace and the more homey the environment, the more time you're apt to spend there *at the expense of* your real home. Remember: Work is for making money, not for emotional satisfaction. Use the money you're making at work to make your home more comfortable and to get more emotional satisfaction from your social, cultural, and spiritual life.

Stay in Constant Circulation

To spot new opportunities you have to be looking. If you're spending all your time doing your current job or running your present business you won't see either your next chance or the signs your current work is about to sink. Spend at least 20 percent of your time looking for and preparing for your next opportunity. That means learning new skills, attending networking functions, going on informational interviews, browsing trade shows, and reading various industry journals. You are a business of one, as I'll discuss in Chapters 5 and 6. And like any other business, to remain successful you have to do constant marketing.

Chat up everyone you meet. Remember: Your path isn't linear any longer. You never know where your next job or business will come from. It's as likely to come from a conversation you have after church or an e-mail exchange on the Sherlock Holmes mailing list on the Internet as it is from schmoozing at an industry function or working a trade show.

Don't Hire Employees

I've already said that employees can be chains that keep you from moving rather than roots that provide security. Everyone working for you should be a temp or an independent contractor . . . and that goes whether you're signing their checks or not. Look for people to work with you rather than for you, individuals whose agendas are at least temporarily complementary to your own. If you have employees you'll not only need to pay them and offer benefits, but you'll naturally worry about them when it comes time to make your next move. That moment's hesitation is all it takes for the window to shut and for you to lose your chance. Similarly, if you have staffers you'll naturally worry about what will happen to them if you want to take on another project or shift companies. Those understandable concerns will just slow you down. Instead, either don't put yourself in that position or make sure those working with you share your attitudes toward work.

Strive for Uniqueness

With all the competition out there you must strive for uniqueness. You can't be just another pizza parlor or just another account executive. There must be something that sets you apart from the pack. You could be the fastest, the most convenient, the best, the most creative, the hippest, the most ethical, the one who offers the most value, or even the most expensive (see Chapter 73), as long as there's something about you or your business that's unique. That's what you'll be selling—the sizzle, not the steak—whether to employers or to customers or to clients.

Develop Relationships

Without a ladder to climb or a set business pattern, relationships take on even more importance. You never know who will be your next customer or your next boss. That doesn't mean you need to befriend everyone you meet. Just don't forget to look down and sideways, as well as up, for contacts and clients. Try to create your own stable of vendors and suppliers, your own roster of regular clients and customers, and your own team of supporting actors. In fact, think of yourself as a film director who has a regular cast of actors, stagehands, writers, producers, and camera people whom he hires and works with. Sometimes you come to them with work, and sometimes they come to you. People should want to work with and for you, and people who hire you should know you'll be bringing quality people along for the ride.

The age of paternalism in the workplace is over. Don't look at people who are doing work for you as your "children." They're not beneath you and you're not above them. You're not responsible for them and they don't need to obey you. You need them to do their work and they need you to pay them fairly for the work they're doing. It's a business relationship, not a family one.

Remember the old adage: Be kind to people on the way up because you'll pass them again on the way down? Well, today you'll be passing them up and down, again and again, so it's even more important to develop and maintain good relationships.

Choose New and Different over More

This is the most vital general principle I can offer you about focusing on change rather than growth. But it's also the most difficult to follow. We've been conditioned to think that more is always better, whether it's more responsibility, more customers, more staff, or more revenue. Today the only "more" that's automatically better is more money in your pocket. And the best way to achieve that is, when confronted by choices, to always opt for the newest or the different path. If it's a choice between taking on more responsibility at work or learning a new skill, choose the new knowledge. Faced with a chance to move into a new market or to expand your share of your existing market? Leap into the new market. Follow "more" instead and you're heading down that old crumbling linear path or up that now rickety hierarchical ladder. You've been conditioned to think it's a path paved with gold. Actually it's the road to ruin.

DEBBIE COOPER CHOOSES CHANGE RATHER THAN GROWTH

Until I suggested it, Debbie Cooper had never thought she could keep her job as marketing vice president at the sportswear manufacturer and start a packaged healthy meal business. I explained to her my concept of setting aside the linear career and business models. She was intrigued. We agreed to meet again in a week and go over ideas about how she could simultaneously keep her job and start her own business.

While I spent that week researching the typical outsourcing opportunities for a catering business, Debbie was more innovative. She came to meet me the next week with the solution. Her sister Michelle was as an even better cook than Debbie. Michelle was currently a stay-at-home married mother of two, living in suburban New Jersey. Debbie had run the idea by her, and Michelle, eager for an opportunity to go into business without having to leave home, was thrilled. The two sisters could collaborate on the recipes. Michelle could then do the actual cooking, freeing Debbie to just do the marketing, which fit in nicely with her exercising. Debbie would still have all the time she needed to do her job and Michelle would have all the time she needed to be a full-time mom. Within a month, Debbie's Triathemeals was born.

Since then the business has flourished. Debbie has gotten dozens of health clubs in the metro area to carry her meals. Michelle has not only taken over production but has contributed some new recipes to the lineup. The sportswear manufacturer still thinks Debbie is the greatest, and she's negotiated two raises. Michelle still gets to go to her daughter's soccer games.

The two women are remaining true to their focus on change rather than growth. They have been approached about opening a restaurant in Greenwich Village and managing the in-house cafés at a chain of health clubs. They've considered both, but turned them down since they would preclude the flexibility they both now think is vital.

WHAT'S NEXT?

Changing your attitudes toward money and work, and learning to focus on change rather than growth, are basically intellectual exercises. For these new beliefs to actually make a difference and enable you to truly work for yourself and to live rich, you need to turn them into actions. That's probably the hardest part of the whole Live Rich program: overcoming your inertia and putting your new attitudes into practice by taking charge of your life. It's also the subject of Chapter 4.

Take Charge

4

You cannot be reactive and live rich. You can set out to make money and focus on change rather than growth, but if you don't take charge, neither shift in attitude will make one bit of difference in your life.

If you don't become proactive, everything you've done up to this point will be no more than an intellectual exercise, something interesting you can discuss over cocktails at your niece's wedding reception. For these changes in attitude and approach to make any difference, you must initiate rather than respond to situations.

It's easy to go through life being reactive. And if you're smart, lucky, and react well, you can actually do okay. But you won't be a winner. This is one instance where life really does mirror sports.

PLAYING THE NEUTRAL ZONE TRAP

In ice hockey there's a defensive strategy called the neutral zone trap. Basically it involves sitting back in a defensive posture, letting the other team come toward your end of the ice. Then you try to force them to make a mistake and turn it into an offensive chance for your team. Teams who play the trap have trouble winning the Stanley Cup. That's because they end up having fewer chances to score than the other team. They need to take advantage of a much higher percentage of their opportunities than the other team does if they want to win.*

---

*The exception that proves this rule occurred when the New Jersey Devils, the foremost practitioners of the neutral zone trap, won the Stanley Cup. However, that season was an unusual one since it was shortened because of a players' strike.

There are people who go through life playing their own version of the neutral zone trap: They sit back and wait for things to happen to them, for opportunities to become available. These are the people who don't go in and ask for a raise; instead, they wait for their boss to come to them. They're the folks who are laid off or fired, rather than the folks who leave for another job.

Being reactive is a good strategy if you just want to be average. That's true in both life and sports. A bad hockey team can become an average one by playing the trap. Similarly, people who wait for things to happen to them might do okay, if they're lucky. They can find out what the manager at McDonald's is looking for in an employee and supply it.

But to become a winner, either at sports or at life, you must be proactive. You need to force the play in the other team's end of the ice so you get more scoring opportunities. You must take chances. You must take charge: Ask for raises on your own; seek out new opportunities while you're still employed. The proactive person sets out to buy a McDonald's franchise, rather than just get a job there.

Sometimes reactive people do well for themselves. Most often, however, they don't become winners. That's because the proactive person has beaten them to the punch. Rather than waiting for a break she has gone out and made her own breaks. Instead of waiting for a door to open, he has kicked it down, and if there wasn't a door, he's cut a hole in the wall and forced his way in. The proactive person has seized the opportunities the reactive person was waiting to appear.

Sure, the proactive person may have to fight through some adversity and struggle out of some valleys, but she has the chance to triumph, to reach the summit, to live rich.

SO WHY DON'T MORE PEOPLE TAKE CHARGE?

I tell all this to my clients when they first come to see me. I encourage them to take charge of their lives. I urge them to seek out opportunities. I tell them to, in the words of Horace, "Seize the day, put no trust in the morrow!" Most nod appreciatively, say they'll start taking charge the moment they leave my office, and yet continue to be reactive. The next time they call it's for help in reacting to a problem. Perhaps they've been laid off. Maybe their business isn't able to meet its bills. Granted, there are some instances when they're calling because something good has happened to them. For instance, they've been offered a promotion or someone has tried to buy out their company. But most times it's a problem. And whatever the case, they're still reacting rather than acting. They're letting things happen to them rather than making things happen.

There are some clients, however, who take my message to heart, who become proactive, who grab life and make it work for them, who end up living rich. In exploring what they were able to do that others couldn't, I've discovered what I think are the two keys to taking charge: not viewing yourself as a victim and not letting your fears get in your way.

Most of my clients who are reactive see themselves as victims or let self-generated fears keep them from success, or both. My proactive clients set aside feelings of victimization, battle through their fears, and take charge of their lives.

A SOCIETY OF VICTIMS

Many Americans see themselves as dysfunctional victims of something or other. About 20 percent of us proudly claim to suffer from a diagnosable psychiatric disorder. There are 25 million "sex addicts." Around 20 million say they're addicted to games of chance. Nearly 50 million say they're depressed enough to need treatment. And while only 20 million say they're alcoholics, another 60 million say they're codependents of alcoholics.

In fact, those in the "codependency" movement say that addictions aren't limited to chemicals or even behavior. They define codependency as a dependency on people, on their moods, their behaviors, their sickness or well-being, and their love. In other words, people who need people are no longer the luckiest people in the world, they're the sickest. To be codependent you no longer have to be the adult child of an alcoholic; you can just be an adult child. Leaders of the codependency movement put the number of victims of this malady at 230 million.*

---

*I have a great deal of respect for most twelve-step programs and I admire those individuals who work to overcome actual addictions. I know how hard that is to do. However, I think identifying yourself as a victim when you're not hurts your chances to Live Rich.

It's Time to Take Responsibility for Your Life

Words are very powerful. By definition a disease is caused by factors beyond our control, and a victim is someone whose situation is the fault of another. If you suffer from a disease or you're a victim, you are not responsible for your condition. Your problem is the fault of a virus, or your parents, or society.

Describing behavior in terms of disease and victimization takes away your control over your life. It says there's no point in taking charge since you're helpless. Saying you suffer from a disease, or calling yourself a victim, disempowers you. Saying you're in control of your life, you're responsible for your own actions, empowers you to take charge and live rich. If you're not responsible for who you are, for what you are, how can you respect yourself? In her book *I'm Dysfunctional, You're Dysfunctional*, Wendy Kaminer notes that "calling the recovery process self-help doesn't change the way it tends to disempower people." Any movement that asks you to "admit you're powerless" is weakening you, not empowering you.

Think about it. Sitting in a room with other adults, clutching a teddy bear, and being told to visualize yourself as a small helpless child is not going to give you a sense of control and a good self-image. You're being infantilized rather than empowered. Rather than being taught to look outward, to mature, and to learn that the world is filled with shades of gray rather than just black and white, you're being encouraged to look inward, return to the womb, and see the world in the black and white terms of a child.

Call yourself diseased or a victim and you can hide from personal responsibility, you can keep from having to take charge. Call yourself whole and triumphant and you have the responsibility to choose what you do and where you go. Having that choice means being free: free to truly work for yourself, free to make money, free to change rather than grow, free to take charge, and free to live rich.

Where Did All These Victims Come From?

America's obsession with victims and victimization began nobly in the 1960s. At that time caring people began to point out that the nation's attitudes and policies created a social climate in which there were victims. The Civil Rights Movement called attention to the plight of African-Americans. Inspired by that success, feminists turned the spotlight on the plight of women. Building on these successes, homosexuals launched the gay rights movement. Then came the elderly and the disabled. Each successive movement saw that there was a segment of the population that was being oppressed, exploited, discriminated against, and, in effect, victimized.

And it wasn't just those on the political left who identified groups of victims. In response to Supreme Court rulings extending the rights of the accused, a crime victims' rights movement was born. In recent years tax protesters, gun owners, and even average taxpayers have begun the metamorphosis into victims' groups.

One of the critical moments in this process came in 1971, when psychologist William Ryan published his book *Blaming the Victim*. Ryan's book focused on his theory that the African-American underclass shouldn't be blamed for street crime and welfare dependency since they were the victims of racial and economic discrimination. Setting the merits of his argument aside, one of its lasting contributions was that it created a process in which victims could be identified without having to identify the victimizers. There was longer a need for a "Bull" Connor. All that was needed was the victim.

While these social changes were taking place, complementary changes were occurring in the mental health industry and the law. Public and private health insurance began paying for mental health services. And with more money to be made, more people began offering those services. Legal reforms made it easier to sue for malpractice and product liability. The more suits that were filed and the higher the compensation—whether through awards or settlements—the more people thought of suing.

All these changes have had such a dramatic effect on America because they've been intentionally or unintentionally supported by what I like to call the "codependency cartel."

The legal system helped because it is, at its very core, concerned with justice and injustice. It is the arena where the claims of injured parties are addressed. And of course, the more of those parties addressing claims, the more powerful and influential the courts become, and the wealthier lawyers become.

Academia has always been the American institution where idealism is most prominent. Is it any wonder then that injustice in any form attracts the attention of both teachers and students? Victims also become the subject of university researchers, paid with grants from those eager to identify, treat, and in some cases potentially profit from victims.

The media love stories of victims. They're dramatic, often involving a single innocent soul being attacked by something large and evil, or at best impersonal. At least superficially they're not ambiguous. That means you don't have to cover both sides. Most times there's some potential solution, even if it's just the hope of therapy. They're popular, and the more people consider themselves potential victims, the more popular stories of victims become. Finally, they're cheap to produce: often just talking heads.

The fourth element of the codependency cartel is the recovery movement: an informal alliance of new age therapeutic practitioners, authors, twelve-step groups, magazine publishers, and conference/ workshop promoters.* More than three hundred stores in this country sell nothing but recovery materials, and there are sections called "recovery" in both feminist and born-again bookstores.

Clearly, most of the recovery movement is well meaning. Therapists aren't charged with finding facts, they're charged with helping others. But, consciously or not, there's also a financial element to the recovery movement labeling us all as victims, just as there's a monetary motive for all the other members of the codependency cartel. When something is declared a disease, that condition enters into a new category, a category that triggers health insurance payments, government and employment benefits, and even special rights and protections under the law. And don't forget about all those books, videos, audiotapes, lectures, workshops, and conferences. In a market-driven society, when dollars stand to be made, there's almost nothing that can stand in the way.

If that was as far as it went, I really wouldn't have a problem with the codependency cartel. If they were all trying to help people, and in the process make an honest buck or two, I'd actually admire them. After all, that's exactly what I'm trying to do in my practice and in my writing. Besides, as you already know, I don't believe in spending lots of time assigning blame. My problem is with the results of all this.

---

*I don't mean to tar and feather all therapists any more than I mean to accuse all lawyers, academics, and members of the media of being part of this cartel. There are many therapists who don't encourage their clients to see themselves as victims. But unfortunately, there are many who do.

The acceptance of this victim ideology by some of my clients is directly keeping them from taking charge of their lives and, as a result, keeping them from living rich.

PROFESSIONAL FEAR REMOVAL

For many years I had a hard time explaining my personal consulting practice. You see, while I'm an attorney, my business isn't strictly a law office. On any one day I'm apt to be simultaneously helping one client get his son into prep school, working to arrange seed financing for another client's new business, negotiating an employment contract for a third client, and scouting for a weekend home for a fourth client. I've been hired to negotiate with multinational corporations, the corner repair shop, and future spouses. In an effort to describe the scope of my practice—careers, real estate, personal finance, consumerism, small business, estate and matrimonial law—I came up with the phrase "the business of living."

While that gave me a workable definition of my practice, I still didn't know how to describe what I did. One of the secrets to being able to offer such comprehensive services—and to do so many things at the same time—is that I don't do everything for my clients. Instead I try to empower clients to do things for themselves. Sure, when there's something technical that requires professional expertise I step in or bring in outside help. I always tell clients that our relationship is a two-way street. I'll do everything I can, but they've got to work at it too. I explain that their success depends more on their own efforts than on mine. My job is to get them to the point where all they need from me is an occasional checkup. So I'm not just an attorney or a financial adviser. I'm more of a teacher/coach/assistant/security blanket. But since that's far too much to put on a business card or letterhead, I was at a loss.

Being unable to find a succinct, accurate definition of myself wasn't just a stationery design problem. As I'll explain in a later chapter, in today's world you need to have just that kind of marketing nugget if you want to succeed. That led me to constantly ask for others' help in trying to come up with a self-definition. After working with a creative client I'd close our postmortem by asking for his ideas on describing what I do. For years all I got were descriptions with lots of slashes. Then one day a publishing person gave me the answer I needed. She looked puzzled when I described my unsuccessful efforts at self-definition. "I'm surprised you've had such trouble," she said. "It's really quite obvious: You're a professional fear remover."*

Fear: The Final Roadblock to Living Rich

I honestly believe we are usually our own worst enemies. Rationally you often know exactly what you need to do to succeed; you realize what you must do to overcome adversity or seize an opportunity. If you don't know the information yourself, others—maybe people like me—tell it to you. Yet you don't always do it. You don't take the advice. You don't take the action.

You're not alone. Far from it. Most people are derailed on their trip to success. Few ever complete the journey. What stops us? Well, for many it's that sense of victimization. But for others it's even simpler: It's fear.

Actually, we often stop ourselves. We're the roadblock that lies between where we are and where we want to be. Fear is the final, seemingly insurmountable hurdle on the sprint toward the life of our dreams. If you've adopted all the other advice I've offered so far in this book—including getting over your victim status—fear is the final thing that can stop you from truly working for yourself and finally living rich.

Understand the Nature of Fear

To be perfectly accurate, I'm not really a fear remover. I don't help people figure out what it is that has caused their fear. I'm not at all concerned about the psychological factors that contribute to your fears of success or failure. All I care about is getting you past them. So I suppose that rather than removing them, I simply disarm them. I do that by suggesting a number of specific techniques outlined at the end of this chapter. But I also do it by getting my clients to understand the nature of their fear. I believe the key is to, in the words of psychologist Susan Jeffers, "feel the fear and do it anyway."†

Fear is something you'll have to deal with for as long as you live. That's because it's an apparently instinctive response to new situations.

---

*She later presented me with a nameplate/business card holder that still sits on the round table I use for a desk. It says "Stephen M. Pollan, professional fear remover."
†That's the title of one of Jeffers's books. Published more than a decade ago, it remains the single best work on the nature of fear and is an outstanding guide to overcoming it. I highly recommend it.

Faced with having to deal with something different or unusual, you get frightened. As long as you continue to confront new situations in life you will continue to experience fear. If you don't want to feel fear, stop experiencing new things. You won't have much of a life—certainly not a rich one—but you'll have stopped feeling fearful.

Why do we get fearful when confronted by something new? It's a self-defense mechanism. The fear forces us to take stock of the situation. It gives us time to develop a response and plan a course of action. The problem is that there are times when we let the fear stop us when it shouldn't. It's okay if, when confronted with a sheer cliff, we pause out of fear, and then decide not to jump. That's fear fulfilling its intended role in our lives. But if, when confronted with an otherwise excellent business opportunity that happens to be in another city, we pause, examine all the ramifications, and let only our fear of something new or different deter us, we're giving fear more power over our lives than is healthy.

Since throughout your life you're always experiencing new things, and therefore always getting fearful, you'd think by middle age you'd be a mass of fears. But, assuming you're normal, you're not. How come? Because those fears go away as soon as you experience whatever it was that was new or different. Let me say that again in other words:

Your fears vanish when you do whatever it was that frightened you.

That's because what was once new and unusual becomes a known quantity. The result of the action doesn't matter. If you don't achieve all you wished, it becomes a learning experience and improves your chances of doing better the next time. You succeed simply by not letting your fear paralyze you. Though I hate to quote a commercial slogan, the secret to overcoming fear is to "just do it." That's what I told Grayson Heinz.

THE STORY OF GRAYSON HEINZ

Grayson Heinz is a thirty-nine-year-old, mild-mannered, urbane young man who wouldn't seem out of place sipping champagne at a gallery opening. By his appearance and manner you'd assume he was a banker. Actually he's in the computer industry. And by all reports he's extremely good at what he does.

Grayson first came to me for a career consultation. A friend of his whom I'd helped with a real estate transaction suggested Grayson see me. At the time Grayson was vice president of an Internet company that had created a "virtual community." He was the second in command and supplied the creativity. The president was the founder and financial person. This fellow was everything Grayson wasn't: aggressive, confrontational, and dictatorial. He was also leaving. That was what brought Grayson in to see me. Grayson wanted help in solidifying his position, advice on making his job safe.

"Forget about shoring up your present spot," I told him, "let's get you the president's position."

"That's really not possible," Grayson responded immediately.

"Why not?" I asked. "You seem like you're the perfect person for the job."

"I'm not," Grayson interjected. "I'm black."

"I can see that," I joked, "but what does that have to do with it?" I asked.

"The president is a racist," Grayson stressed.

"Grayson," I said sternly, "don't let yourself be victimized by prejudice."

FORGET THE "HOW," CONCENTRATE ON THE "NOW"

I'm sure there are some who, having read Grayson's story, will accuse me of "blaming the victim." Ever since William Ryan coined that phrase it has been the charge that can stop any contrarian or politically incorrect argument in its tracks. But in this case it's just plain wrong. Nor am I "in denial," to use the blanket condemnation the members of the recovery movement use to paint anyone who doesn't join them in admitting he's diseased or a victim.

Taking charge in no way minimizes or denies any real injuries you may have suffered in your life. Nor does it say your fears aren't justified. I'm not denying there's racism, sexism, homophobia, anti-Semitism, or any other of the all too many hatreds in the world. There clearly are people addicted to alcohol, tobacco, and drugs. I'm not saying there's no discrimination against the disabled or that there's no child abuse. (I'm not so sure about UFO abductions and Satanic ritual abuse, however . . . but that's for another book.) People suffer from all these terrible things, and more. There may well be someone or something to blame for what happened to you in the past. And it's entirely natural to be afraid of new or different situations. Everyone feels the same fear of the unknown. In other words, your anger and your fear could be entirely justified.

But fear and anger will do nothing for you now. And that's what counts: the now. How you got to where you are stopped mattering the moment you got there. And the fear you feel matters only during the time it takes for you to contemplate an action. After that, blame belongs to the past and fear becomes moot. I'm not saying you should forget about the past. And I'm not entirely sure you should forgive either (although it might be good for your soul in the long run). Nor am I saying you shouldn't feel fear. What I'm suggesting to you, and what I tell my clients, is that the assigning of blame should have no bearing on what you do from this point on, and fear shouldn't be allowed to stop you.

Get out from between your ears—it's a bad neighborhood. You may have been victimized, but you become a victim only if you let the past be the focus of your life. You fail only if you let fear stop you. You can beat those demons from the past and overcome your fears by getting on with the "now," by taking charge of your present life. Wallow in the "how" and you let the demons and fears win. You have free will. You can pursue your goals. You can live rich . . . like Grayson Heinz.

GRAYSON HEINZ GETS OUT FROM BETWEEN HIS EARS

When Grayson told me that he couldn't get the president's job at the Internet company because he was African-American I listened sympathetically. Grayson explained the subtle racism he'd sensed from the members of the board. He described the not-so-subtle racism of his boss, generally consisting of unfunny jokes and inappropriate comments.

I told Grayson I shared his anger, but that it was an impotent emotion. I said that it seemed to me, albeit from a distance, that the president's and the board's racism would likely stop at their bottom line. I explained that I thought he was considering himself a victim, and launched into the argument I've made in this chapter. I told Grayson that if he didn't go after the president's position he was solidifying his victim status. But if he went after the job he would be taking charge and on the road to living rich. I must have been really on that day, because it didn't take more than half an hour for me to bring Grayson around to my view.* We then came up with a plan to get the job.

Grayson drafted a report outlining exactly what he would do as president, spelling out the changes he'd make, describing the directions he'd take the online community the company had created, and establishing a timetable for achieving his profitability goals. He approached the job not as an employee asking for an entitlement but as a consultant pitching a long-term project. The board members were shocked and impressed. The former president was stunned into silence. Not only was Grayson's report outstanding, but his presentation and demeanor showed he could do the job. And not incidentally, his newfound assertiveness subtly indicated that he wasn't likely to stick around if he didn't get the position. As I'd suspected, profits overcame prejudice, and Grayson got the job.

Since that time Grayson has been the epitome of a take-charge person. He has kept one step ahead in his career. He knew the company was overly reliant on one advertiser and so early on drafted a plan to broaden its revenue stream, adding advertisers and a subscription fee. He presented his plan as soon as it was completed . . . which turned out to be just two months before that big advertiser failed to renew its schedule. What would have been a disaster became a triumph. Rather than hurting him, the situation solidified his position. Since then he has followed the same pattern, always acting as if he were an outside consultant hired by the company.

Grayson's success has drawn attention not just from the parent company but from other Internet companies. He has translated that attention into substantial salary increases and an equity position. Rather than giving the company ownership of his creativity and insight, he's leasing it to them. At the moment he's considering actually becoming the outside consultant he has modeled himself after.

Grayson says he's happier than he's ever been in his life. He has bought a weekend home and helped his wife set up her own business. He is truly working for himself, and as a result he's living rich.

---

*I'd like to think Grayson's conversion was so quick because I'm so persuasive. However, it could have been that, deep down, he was ready for this message. In the end it doesn't matter. What counts is that he got the job.

GETTING OUT OF YOUR OWN HEAD

How can you replicate Grayson's success? Well, unfortunately there's no easy formula for getting out of your own head. It takes real work to buck the trend and take responsibility for your life. It's tough to "feel the fear and do it anyway." Most of the exertion, thankfully, is mental. Here are some ideas that have helped my clients:

Change Your Definition of Success

Have you ever not taken an action because you were afraid of what would happen if you didn't succeed? Well, it's time to change your definition of success, to update it for the twenty-first century. For whatever reason, baby boomers have learned that to succeed they must be perfect. But perfection is not the only measure of success, and it's certainly not the one to use in our current environment.

The greatest batters in baseball hit successfully less than 40 percent of the time. In fact, if they hit successfully 30 percent of the time over the course of a long career they're solid candidates for the Hall of Fame.

Perfection isn't achievable, and viewing it as the measure of success will lead only to frustration and immobilizing fear. You're not perfect. No one is. In fact, it's your imperfections that make you a human being, that give you a uniqueness, that give you character. It's those imperfections that enable you to love and be loved.

Success and failure mean different things for those who live rich than for those who live poor. Those who live rich know that failure comes only from *not* taking an action. If you take an action and the result isn't as good as you hoped, you've still succeeded. That's because you've changed—remember Chapter 3? By changing you've gained experiences and created new opportunities for yourself. It's movement that's the key to work in the twenty-first century, whether that means taking a step forward, backward, or sideways. The status quo and stagnation are what you must avoid at all costs. Movement of any kind equals change, and change of any kind equals success.

If you find yourself hesitating, giving in to the fear, visualize the worst thing that could happen if you take the action. I'll bet that your worst-case scenario is far more horrible than is called for. The actual results of falling short of perfection are almost never as bad as we ourselves imagine. Verbalize those scenarios. Share them with others. Get feedback. I'll bet you'll soon find they're irrational. Remember: In work, the results of inaction are almost certainly worse than any possible results of action.

Stop Being Your Own Worst Enemy

Have you ever not taken an action because you thought you somehow weren't capable of it or deserving of the possible reward? It's incredible, but we often do things to ourselves we would never let others do to us.

Do you criticize yourself? Would you let others get away with saying the things about you that you're thinking about yourself? If not, then stop thinking them. Become an ally to yourself, not an enemy.

How are you treating your subordinates or peers? Do you offer them praise for a job well done? Do you thank them for their efforts, regardless of the outcome? Do you give them a pat on the back when they're feeling down? I'm sure you do. Then why don't you do the same for yourself? Treat yourself as well as you treat everyone else.

Being nice to yourself doesn't mean you're an egomaniac or a pompous ass. It means you're a healthy, well-adjusted person with a realistic, not an inflated, ego. It means you're not shooting yourself in the foot. It means you're ready, willing, and able to live rich.

If you want to start your own business, don't tell yourself you don't have what it takes. If your current business hasn't done as well as you'd hoped, don't call yourself a failure. If you've been laid off or passed over, don't think of yourself as a loser. Treat yourself as you would anyone else in that situation. Praise yourself for everything you've done well. Then identify any mistakes you made and fill in any gaps you've discovered. Then get back up on that horse.

Judge Your Progress, Not Your Results

Don't give up because you're not at the place you think you should be. You are just where you are supposed to be. Stop measuring yourself against everyone else. There will always be someone who has a larger home, who drives a more expensive car, who makes more money, who has a higher-paying job, or whose business generates more profits. There will also always be someone who has a smaller home than you, whose car is in worse shape than yours, who makes less money than you do, who's under you in the hierarchy, or whose business isn't doing as well as yours.

You shouldn't feel bad about yourself because there's someone with more than you. And you shouldn't feel good about yourself because there's someone less fortunate. Judge your personal progress rather than your outward trappings. Are you moving toward meeting your own real needs? If the answer is yes, you're doing fine. If the answer is no, you're off track. All you need to do is start moving toward your goals.

The guy driving the Jaguar who isn't truly working for himself isn't going to feel like he's living rich. He's working to outdo his neighbors and to show his father that he's better than the old man thought. The woman driving the Geo who is truly working for herself will feel far richer. She's working from home, banking more than she did when she was a corporate executive, and simultaneously seeing her son grow up. Believe me, I know. I meet them both (or at least people like them) all the time.

Living rich isn't a zero-sum game. Someone else's success doesn't minimize your chances, and someone else's failure doesn't improve your odds. When it comes to living rich we're all playing solitaire.

Don't worry about how your salary measures up to all the other forty-five-year-old accountants you know. Don't compare your catering business's profitability to that of every other caterer in town. Instead compare where you are with where you want to be. If you're heading in the right direction, you're fine. The only measuring stick that matters is that you're truly working for yourself. Then, and only then, will you feel like you're living rich.

Life Is Not Ad Hoc: Set Achievable Goals

Do you find yourself not taking an action because you're not sure where you want to go? Or do you feel frustrated and give up because your goals are so far away?

Life isn't ad hoc. You can't expect to achieve goals if you haven't established them. And you can't take charge unless you've set priorities. The broad outline of your plan is obvious: to truly work for yourself. And your primary goal is clear: to live rich. Now just fill in the details. Determine your own real needs. Make sure you're truly working for yourself. Concentrate on how you can make money. Focus on ways you can change rather than just grow.

If you move through life without a plan you're relying on fate, luck, or someone else's intervention to live rich. You're acting as a helpless victim rather than an empowered individual. Do not cede control over your life. There's nothing contradictory about believing in both God's power and your own power. You have free will.

At the same time, make sure the goals you set are achievable as well as your own. It's okay to reach a bit beyond your grasp (else what's a heaven for?) but make sure they're still within lunging distance. If you're not sure whether you're being realistic, speak to someone who'd know. If you set unrealistic goals you'll end up falling short, getting frustrated, and giving up. Set realistic, achievable goals and you'll meet them, get inspired, and continue to take charge of your life.

Concentrate on the Rowing, Not the Steering

You've established your goals and priorities. Now put your head down and start rowing toward them just as hard as you can. Don't worry about the navigation, however.

Remember: In the twenty-first century there's no longer a set career ladder or business path. No one, least of all you, can predict what your voyage will be like. You know where you're starting and where you want to end up. The rest is unpredictable. You've written the prologue and the final scene; now forget about penning the rest of the script. Be the star actor, not the writer/director.

Will you always arrive where you intended? In all honesty, no. Sometimes you'll come up short and sometimes you'll exceed your wildest dreams. Sometimes you'll end up in places you never expected. Your only set destination is a rich life. And if you truly work for yourself you'll get there, whether or not it looks the way you anticipated. It really is the journey that matters . . . as long as you're living rich along the way.

Raise Your Sails to Catch More Wind

Do you not take an action because you're afraid of taking a chance? Well, go ask any group of older people about their regrets. I'll guarantee you hear one recurring theme: They wish that they'd taken more chances in life, that they hadn't played things so safe, that they weren't so conservative in their life choices and decisions, that they hadn't given in to their fears so often.

Life and work follow the same universal principle as investing: Risk and reward are inseparable. If you want to live life to the fullest you have to take some chances. You can't live rich without taking some risks.

That doesn't mean life should be a series of constant gambles. Just as investors study and strategize and measure risks, so should you. Play the odds. Look for opportunities. Have a safety net. Understand life's markets. Accept that you can't win the game unless you play. If you lead your life as a savings account investor you'll live safe, but you'll never live rich. That doesn't mean you have to live your life as a stock picker. You should be more like a mutual fund investor: in the market, taking measured risk.

Rather than gambling, you're simply raising your sails higher to catch more wind. Be open to more opportunities. Be willing to take some chances. Don't lock doors shut without first looking inside and seeing where they lead. You only live once . . . as far as I know. If you're going to live rich you've got to reach for the brass ring. If you don't you'll live to regret it.

A CHAIN REACTION

Living rich is the end result of a series of actions. Taken separately they each make sense both financially and emotionally. But taken together their power is multiplied tenfold. They start a chain reaction, a surge of empowerment that can change your world.

The exact actions you take will vary depending on your own situation. But in general, once you stop looking at yourself as a victim and overcome your fears you'll be able to take charge and move off the ledge of indecision, inaction, and reactive behavior. You'll then be able to make money and focus on change rather than growth. Having gotten those balls rolling you'll truly be working for yourself. And soon you'll feel like you're finally living rich.

I think we've all been looking for a magic bullet—a single answer for how to live rich—for so long we've missed the obvious. There is no single cure for the work malaise that afflicts us; there is no wonder drug that can, in a single dose, save us; there is no one magic secret to living rich. None of the steps or attitudes I've outlined is miraculous alone. But if you adopt them as a philosophy and apply them to your work life you'll experience an incredible chain reaction, the results of which are truly extraordinary.

Clients of mine who are employees are always shocked when I explain that being self-employed doesn't mean you're truly working for yourself. Entrepreneur clients, on the other hand, know exactly what I mean.

When you own and operate your own business—whether it consists solely of you or has a hundred employees—you soon realize the business has a propensity to take on a life of its own. The entrepreneur worries about how the business is doing. What do others think of the business? Is it healthy? Is it getting all the revenue it needs to grow up big and strong? Is it moving in the right direction? Am doing all I can for it? Am I being a good owner?

ENTREPRENEUR AS PARENT

The only relationship comparable to entrepreneur/business is that of parent/child. This entrepreneur-as-parent parallel makes a lot of sense. After all, a business is the creation of the entrepreneur. A business springs from the entrepreneur's head just as a child springs from its parents' loins. As the fruit of personal creation it becomes the repository for all sorts of emotional and psychological baggage. Just as a child, for better or worse, becomes part of a parent's identity, so a business becomes part of the entrepreneur's identity. And just as some parents live their lives vicariously through their children, so many entrepreneurs live their work lives vicariously through their businesses. They assume the success of the business automatically translates into their own personal success.

A child reaches adulthood and, while legally emancipated, remains the emotional, psychological, and moral responsibility of the parent. So too a business can be incorporated—in effect, becoming a legal entity of its own—but remain the embodiment of the entrepreneur's dreams. And just as parents sometimes put their grown child's interests ahead of their own, so entrepreneurs often put their business's interests first. Just ask Mike O'Shea.

THE STORY OF MIKE O'SHEA

Mike O'Shea is a fascinating young man. Funny, brilliant, and charming, he looks like a dark-haired Jimmy Cagney. The only child of a policeman and schoolteacher, Mike excelled in school. He graduated from Rutgers University and entered New York University's Law School. He excelled there as well, and emerged from law school in 1976 as a rising star. Some of New York's top law firms competed for him, resulting in his getting an incredible starting salary. From his first day at the big firm he'd joined, he was marked as a man to watch. But sometimes, when things come too fast, they have a way of not working out.

Since he was being groomed as a rainmaker (someone who brings new business into a law firm) Mike was never really burdened with the kind of grunt work most legal associates face. He *was* spending long hours on the job. However, I wouldn't call what he was doing working. He was busy wining and dining current and prospective clients, taking them to concerts, ball games, plays, and, since it was the 1970s, nightclubs. Being the youngest rainmaker, Mike was assigned the youngest clients—those from the worlds of entertainment and consumer electronics. You can probably guess what happened. As Mike now jokes, "Cocaine is God's way of telling you you're making too much money."

Mike's fall was as meteoric as his rise. He went from being on top of the world to out on the street in four short years. Fired from the firm because of his drug problem, he had few options open to him. To his credit, he checked himself into a treatment program. When he came out six months later, he moved back in with his parents in suburban

New Jersey. "I felt like I was living out a sad Bruce Springsteen song," he jokes. But the song wasn't over.

Realizing he'd never be able to reenter the partnership track at a big firm, Mike decided to go into business for himself. Rather than hanging out a shingle in the suburbs, Mike borrowed money from his parents and bought a cellular telephone, a laptop computer, and a first-class plane ticket to Los Angeles. He reactivated his contacts in the entertainment world. A young musician he'd befriended back in the 1970s had become a hot record producer. He steered Mike to some artists who needed representation. Bit by bit, working primarily from a hotel room and a rented Miata, Mike started building a law practice.

Six months later he was back in New York. His two music industry clients provided him with enough cash flow to rent a small office on Manhattan's Upper East Side and to hire an office assistant. He soon landed his first theater client—a Broadway director. She led him to his first film client—a cinematographer. Month by month his business grew. Eighteen months after starting the practice he hired another lawyer. A year after that another attorney joined his firm. When I met him, six years after he got out of rehab, his practice had grown from a one-man operation grossing $50,000 to a ten-person business with revenues of $3 million.

Mike came to me for a business consultation. "Why do you need my help?" I asked him. "You seem to be doing great."

He corrected me: "The *business* is doing great. *I'm* doing lousy." Mike said he felt like a slave to his business. He was working from 6 A.M. to 10 P.M., and while revenues were soaring, his own income and lifestyle were not. It's not that he missed the night life of the 1970s— he just wanted to have the time to find Ms. Right. I told him I knew just what he needed to do. "You've got to disown your business."

DISOWNING YOUR OWN BUSINESS

Your business shouldn't be an extension of yourself. It's not your child, it's your business. Your business should be nothing more than a tool for profit. It shouldn't be an entity in and of itself. You may have incorporated it for sound legal and tax reasons (a decision and process we'll discuss in later chapters), but that doesn't mean it should really take on a life of itself and become immortal.

A business may spring from your mind, but it's not your child.

Treat your business as a child and you start doing things for it, rather than for you. In treating your business like a human being you turn it into a monster. You start worrying about how it's doing rather than how you're doing. You start focusing on its growth rather than your wallet. You start thinking of its image rather than your lifestyle. You start worrying about its future rather than your present. And the more you do this, the more you'll have to do it. The business will thrive on this kind of attention. You'll see that and continue your efforts. The business will grow fat feeding on your energy and effort. It will never have enough of your time. It will always want more from you, demanding you service it twenty-four hours a day, seven days a week. It feeds on your energy. Meanwhile you're withering and waning.

Instead, your business should exist solely to satisfy your own real needs. It should have no needs of its own . . . at least none you should care about. You shouldn't worry about what's needed to grow the business, only what's needed to grow your income. If the two are complementary, that's great. But if they're not, concentrate on your income and let the business wither instead.

A business is a means to an end, not an end in itself. And the end you care about is living rich, not becoming chairman of a multinational corporation. F. W. Woolworth created a huge business. But by all reports, despite the material success with which he surrounded himself, he didn't live rich. Like most entrepreneurs, he was working for the company, not for himself. The business certainly thrived. It grew and blossomed and spread around the world for decades after its founder died a wealthy but unhappy man, leaving wealthy and unhappy heirs.

To live rich you need to disown the business child you've spawned. You must cut your emotional and psychological ties to it. Remember: You now need to change quickly and make the most money possible. That may mean sucking the lifeblood (cash) out of a business and leaving it dead on the side of road, or shifting your attention from one opportunity that may have peaked to another. You wouldn't treat a pet that way, let alone a child.

The answer is to never form that kind of attachment in the first place, or if you have, to sever it. By refusing to treat your business like a human being, you keep it from turning into a monster. That's what I've done in my own business.

DISOWNING MY OWN BUSINESS

Sometimes it's very hard to practice what you preach. I've been telling my entrepreneur clients to disown their businesses for years. But it's only since I started working on this book that I realized I hadn't followed my own advice.

I started my current business fifteen years ago. When it began it was a shoestring operation. I was the only full-time employee and I operated out of my co-op apartment. But as my practice grew, the lean business began gaining weight. At first it was muscle. I hired two part-time people—Martin Ruddoy, a lawyer who was trying to become a comedian, and Jane Morrow, who was going to law school—and installed them in a converted bedroom in my apartment. I worked out of the dining room.

When neighbors started complaining to the co-op board I was forced to move operations to an outside location. Martin left to pursue comedy full-time. (Successfully, I'm happy to add. He has become a joke writer for Jay Leno, among others.) Jane came with me. (When she graduated law school she became my associate.) We also hired someone to handle the telephones and do assorted office tasks, freeing up Jane and me.

That single full-time assistant eventually became two people: an assistant and a paralegal. Those two became three: an assistant, a paralegal, and a bookkeeper. Those three became four: an assistant, a paralegal, a bookkeeper, and an office manager to supervise them all. Eventually, while the revenue from the practice grew, profitability didn't keep pace. I was working harder than ever before, but I wasn't seeing any more in my pocket.

I was coming in at seven-thirty every morning and working on the weekend. Other than Jane, no one else arrived before nine or took work home. Sure, it was my business, not theirs, but it seemed like I was working hard to pay for that assistant, that paralegal, that bookkeeper, and that office manager, rather than for myself. When revenues dropped during an off month, their incomes all stayed the same while mine dropped. During a couple of poor months I actually started using revenue from other sources to pay the business's bills. Who was working for whom? I started to wonder. I certainly wasn't working for myself anymore. Despite my best efforts the business had taken on a life of its own. I was working for it. It was no longer working for me. I resolved to start disowning the business.

CREATE YOURSELF.COM

How do you disown your own business? There are number of specific pragmatic steps you need to take, all of which are outlined in the entrepreneurial chapters in the second part of this book. Some of them include:

Outsourcing everything other than your core function.

Minimizing your roots in real space.

Replacing staffers with either independent contractors or other entrepreneurs.

Leasing or renting, rather than owning, all hard assets.

Focusing on your personal profitability rather than the company's bottom line.

Offering new products or services to your current market.

Seeking out new markets to enter.

Cutting loose a business when profitability drops.

Jumping into a new business while the former business is still generating revenue.

I've done almost all of these in my own business. I'll discuss the specifics in the relevant chapters in Part II. However, before you can do any of these specific things, you need to change your attitude toward your business: You have to replace the parent/child model of entrepreneurship with a new one, a concept I call Yourself.com.

Instead of viewing your business as a child, establish—in thought if not in action—your own personal company. This is a company of one—you—that represents solely your own real needs. Yourself.com is the umbrella through which you earn money. Through it you can start or buy new profitable businesses, kill off or sell old ones, or perhaps even form a joint venture with another organization or even an employer for a time. What's key is that Yourself.com never has any agenda other than your personal needs and wants.

The degree to which Yourself.com takes on a separate legal form depends on your own unique situation. While I encourage every entrepreneur to incorporate (see Chapter 28), there may be valid financial, legal, or tax reasons for your operations to take some other form.

More important than the actual legal structure of your operations is that you start looking at your businesses as ways to make the money you need to live rich. Each individual business has a lifespan determined entirely by its moneymaking ability. Since you'll be focusing on change rather than growth you'll always be ready to pursue new opportunities that offer the chance to make more money. At times you'll have just one business contributing money to Yourself.com. In other instances you may have two: one whose moneymaking potential has peaked and is perhaps on the way down, and another that you're nurturing to take its place. There are some entrepreneurs who may even be able to keep three or more businesses up and running simultaneously: one on rise, one that's tailing off, and one or two that are steady moneymakers requiring only minimal effort to keep going. That's Mike O'Shea's situation.

MIKE O'SHEA.COM

Intellectually, Mike was quick to grasp and agree with my advice about disowning his business. Emotionally, however, it took him a few months. His business was psychologically tied up with his comeback and recovery. He knew it was irrational, but he was afraid that without the business he'd fall back into addiction. The final straw came when he spent all that Christmas Eve and Christmas Day in the office. He realized that he had given up his entire personal life for the business. Far from living rich, he was living poorer than when he was in the treatment center. There, at least, he had time to celebrate the holidays with his family and friends.

During a two-hour meeting with me the weekend before New Year's Day, Mike mapped out how he would disown his business and start Mike O'Shea.com. When the office reopened after the holidays, he held a staff meeting. He announced that he was splitting up the company. He would be taking the theater and publishing clients as his own, and he offered the music and film clients to the two other attorneys respectively. Mike asked that they each pay him a percentage of their fees from those clients for two years. He said he would be going back to working out of his apartment, and asked his personal assistant to continue in that position. He told the other attorneys they could assume the lease on the office and maintain the remaining staff as their own, in exchange for a onetime lump sum payment. After two months of negotiations between the parties, the split took place.

Today Mike O'Shea.com has three different income streams. He is now adding a business consulting service to Mike O'Shea.com, which he thinks will eventually take the place of the income he's still getting from the other two attorneys. His personal net income has actually gone up since he disowned the company. More important, he freed up the time to get reinvolved in his church, has met a lovely young lady, and is hoping to get married. For the first time in his life, he's truly working for himself—not for his parents, a law firm, or his business—and as a result, he's living rich.

DON'T IGNORE CHAPTER 6

I'm sure your natural inclination as an impatient entrepreneur is to skip over Chapter 6 and move right into the specifics of Part II. Please don't. It's likely that sometime in the future operations of Yourself.com you'll end up on someone's payroll, even if only part-time or for a year, while you're changing from one business to another. That means you'll need to know how to live rich as an employee.

Become a Mercenary

6

The world of employment has changed forever. That's not news to anyone who has been conscious for the past decade.

The Great Downsizing first began in response to a recessionary economy. Few of my clients took much notice of it—after all, blue-collar workers had always been subject to layoffs when the business cycle slowed. But soon people began to notice that it wasn't just "the usual suspects" who were getting the pink slips. Layoffs began to reach into the ranks of white-collar middle management. However, most assumed it was an aberration—it would just be the unlucky few who were working for firms with one foot in the grave who would lose their jobs. But it was actually the warning sign, the first blip on the radar screen, of an impending sea change.

THE LOYAL FOOT SOLDIER GETS SCREWED

For years American businesses had built up very hierarchical structures with all sorts of middle managers, department heads, and division directors. From a societal view this was necessary: It created jobs for all those highly educated baby boomers who were entering the job market. However, as competition became global, and as information technology was introduced, such hierarchical structures became handicaps.

Small companies were quick to take advantage of information technology and could soon do things that previously required large (and costly) organizations. Since they didn't have multilayered bureaucracies to support they could charge less for comparable goods and services. Information technology also enabled foreign businesses to compete with American firms. Their lower pay standards offered them competitive advantages.

In an effort to compete with smaller and foreign businesses, America's largest corporations starting cutting staff. Every time they laid off a few thousand souls, Wall Street applauded. Soon it became a reflex: Layoff equaled higher stock prices. Since most corporate executives have their personal compensation tied to stock prices, in one way or another, they were helping themselves as they helped the company and its stockholders. The losers in all this were the employees. Our entry into a new world became obvious when America's most paternalistic employer laid off 40,000 loyal IBMers.

Brought up to believe in an unwritten contract that said they'd keep their jobs if they were loyal foot soldiers and did their duty, and would get raises if they stuck around, and would advance if they reenlisted and got seniority, employees were faced with a new world. Suddenly neither performance nor longevity nor seniority meant anything. There was no security, not even for the most loyal of soldiers. There were no automatic pay increases. There was no ladder to climb. The rug had been pulled out from under employees' feet. They were rudderless. They had no foundation. They had done everything they'd been told—they'd followed their orders to the letter—yet they were being let go.

Workplace pundits are offering hundreds of suggestions—some savvy, some silly—about how employees can deal with the changing economy and come out on top. Many, including myself in *Die Broke*, have urged employees to think of themselves like free agent athletes— the employees who have probably done the best in this new, laissez-faire type of environment. I still think the free agent analogy works for those who have specific talents that remain in demand, and who can negotiate pay based on their past performance. But I've seen in my own practice that not everyone is a twenty-five-year-old left-handed pitcher who won twenty games last year. Some people are thirty-five-year-old utility infielders who batted .240. These folks are still valuable—no team can win without them—but they're not going to command the kind of attention that merits their behaving like free agents.

THE STORY OF VINCE LARUSSO

Vince LaRusso thanks God every day for his job. Even though he went to school to study accounting, he never wanted to become a CPA—he thought it would be boring. Fresh out of college he got a job in the business department of a media conglomerate. Vince worked with budgeting and helped negotiate contracts with vendors. While his specific job wasn't the most exciting thing around, Vince got a thrill from being involved in the media business. He was good at his job, and when the company announced the formation of a new venture—an innovative cable television channel—Vince was offered the spot as its business manager. He jumped at the opportunity.

That was ten years ago. Since then Vince's cable channel has become a fixture in the American landscape. It's as recognizable as any of the major television networks. And while Vince's responsibilities still include mundane tasks like budgeting and contract negotiations, his role has expanded to include picking new business opportunities for the channel.

Vince first came to see me two years ago. In response to raids from other organizations, the parent company had issued an edict that executives above a certain level would from then on need to sign employment contracts. I had helped two other executives at the channel negotiate their contracts, and they recommended that Vince see me. Even after he arrived at my office, he was hesitant. "I don't want to do anything to jeopardize my job," he said before we even sat down. "This is my dream job. The only reason I'm here is Bob and Stan [my other two clients] made me promise I'd get some advice." Vince stressed that, while his two friends were in the creative side of the business and were therefore in much demand, as business manager he wasn't ever going to be a star in the media business.

"That may be," I said, "but you've still got wise friends. However much you love your job, and whether or not you consider yourself a star, you've got to stop acting the loyal foot soldier and instead become a mercenary."

THE CONDOTTIERE

Today's employment environment parallels an earlier time, another period when the ordinary foot soldier was being thrown to the wolves at the whim of his leader and when the existing social order had crumbled. Of course, at that time the soldiers could literally be thrown to wolves, and the social order was feudalism.

In the Middle Ages, Europe was embroiled in conflicts large and small. Most countries relied on drafting peasants into their armies. The king would ask his dukes for help. The dukes would ask their subservient lords for help. The lords, who owned most if not all the land, went around their townships and gathered as many of their tenant farmers as they could catch. The crowd of conscripted peasants marched off to fight for their king.

When the conflict revolved around something that mattered to the majority of the population—perhaps religion, or maybe national pride—the draftees went along with a minimum of grumbling. And if their leaders, from the king on down, rewarded them for their fighting, they might even be enthusiastic. But as these feudal wars dragged on for many of years it became clear that the conflicts had little or nothing to do with the people or their lives. Worse yet, the loyal foot soldiers never seemed to get a reward for fighting and often dying for their king and country. By the middle of the fourteenth century, the social order was collapsing.

In northern and central Italy city-states like Venice, Milan, and Florence were trying to come up with a way to address this problem. Being primarily urban, they had always had a hard time raising armies, since they didn't have the feudal landlord/tenant system to fall back on. At the same time, skilled soldiers were looking for a way to be rewarded for their efforts, a system that would guarantee them an income. Together the two groups came up with a system that fit their own real needs. Rather than relying on some unwritten social contract, they drafted actual legal contracts.

The city-states began hiring people to fight for them. They issued contracts to soldier/entrepreneurs. Since the word for contract was *condotta,* these soldiers were called condottiere. (In England these independent professional soldiers were called free lances.) Usually a city would contract with a well-known military leader to serve as its general. He in turn would hire individual captains, who headed up bands of professional soldiers. The contracts on every level were very specific, spelling out the number and type of troops to be provided, how long they would serve, and, most important, how much they would be paid.

Historians have mixed feelings about these mercenaries. On the one hand, condottiere were sometimes more interested in getting paid than actually fighting—particularly if they were going to be fighting other condottiere. After all, you don't want to get on the bad side of future potential employers or coworkers. Some wars involving condottiere involved more maneuvering and clever ruses than actual combat.

On the other hand, the condottiere brought professionalism to warfare. As long as they were paid, the condottiere were much more reliable and honorable than peasant armies. They didn't have to loot and pillage. They had a professional code of conduct and ethics. They formed their own business units and showed remarkable group cohesion, unlike the hordes of peasants. Since their incomes relied on their providing quality to their customers, they developed their skills and worked on their efficiency. It's the condottiere who are credited with being the first to actually seriously study and write about the "art of war." Some condottiere signed long-term contracts with city-states, becoming standing armies of independent contractors rather than temps hired just for the duration of a crisis.

The condottiere were answerable ultimately only to themselves, responsible for their own security and safety, for their own growth of skills, their own savings, their own futures. Rather than leaving themselves at the mercies of their lord employers, they took charge of their own work lives. If you want to live rich it's the professional, self-sufficient condottiere mercenaries who should be your model, not the lowly helpless peasant draftee.

BECOME A MERCENARY

The chapters throughout Part II of this book are filled with specific examples of how you can become a mercenary. For now, let me just go over some general principles.

Security Comes Only from Within

It's crazy to rely on your employer to provide security. The age of the paternalistic employer is over. Even Japanese companies are terminating staff. Ironically, by viewing yourself as a mercenary, free from allegiance to any one company, you can find security. That's because security today comes from having the mental and physical freedom to find and exploit opportunities, wherever they may be. And it's that kind of freedom that lets you live rich.

Think Like a Free Lance

Just as the condottiere were always on the lookout for new cities or countries who needed a lance-for-hire, so you must always be looking for new opportunities, inside and outside your company. Look for unmet needs. Figure out how you can apply your skills (or acquire the skills needed) to meet them. And let people know you're available. That could mean moonlighting on occasion, or perhaps taking on some outside projects, if you can't find new markets in your company. Eventually it might even mean finding an entirely new company or starting one of your own. You shouldn't put your entire 401(k) in the stock of one company. Neither should you put your whole future in the hands of one employer.

Embrace Uncertainty

The condottiere were never sure who they'd next be fighting with, for, or against. Their lives were full of uncertainty. But they compensated by developing other areas of certainty in their lives, primarily their identification with a profession, their skills, and, for many, their religion. Make workplace uncertainty less disconcerting by cultivating certainty in other areas of your life: your home, family, friends, hobbies, and faith, for instance.

Become a Student

The condottiere were always studying the latest innovations and developments in their field. They were students of war and warfare. So you must become a student of your company, your industry, and your profession. You need to be able to discern where your company's needs will arise before they're evident to everyone. You must be able to spot trends in your industry before they make the front page of a trade journal. You have to keep abreast of the latest developments in your profession so you're always considered an expert at what you do.

Promote Yourself

It wasn't enough for the condottiere to let their actions speak for themselves. To drum up more business they needed to promote themselves, to let other city-states know of their successes. They also needed to establish measurable objectives—say, capturing a citadel— so they could demonstrate success to their current and future employers. You need to promote yourself inside and outside your organization by developing your own banners covered with battle honors—whether they take the form of brochures or Web pages. And you need to establish clear-cut goals so you can demonstrate success to your employer in justification of a salary increase, or to show a track record of achievements to a future employer. The condottiere sold themselves by showing the benefits they'd bring their employers. You should do the same.

Develop Professional Pride

It's important to be proud of what you do. But it's also important to take pride in something that's lasting and truly valuable. The condottiere took pride not in the ever-changing nations and city-states that might rule their homeland, but in their individual skills. They had professional pride. That's where you should place your pride. Forget being an organization man. The organization gave up on you (and every other employee) more than a decade ago. It's time you gave up on it. The organization is a parent who disowned you. Rather than spending the rest of your life trying to earn back its love and devotion, look to yourself. The company may be the only work parent you've ever known. But if you stay in that relationship, if you let yourself be treated like dirt by an uncaring employer, you'll never be able to live rich. Take pride in yourself, in your own professionalism, rather than in your being an employee of a particular firm in a specific industry. That's the way to truly work for yourself and to live rich.

VINCE LARUSSO UNFURLS HIS OWN BANNER

Vince wasn't at all eager to become a mercenary. He was a company man. If the cable channel had an employee uniform he would have worn it on weekends as well. If the cable channel had a company pledge he'd have recited it each and every morning. I figured I'd take a more gradual approach, and so just concentrated on negotiating the terms of his employment contract. It was tough going. Vince didn't want to make waves. It was almost as if he was willing to pay the company to work there, if that would ensure keeping his job.

That all changed three weeks after our first meeting. I got a call from one of my other clients at the cable channel. Bob told me he had been terminated. In fact, his entire project group had been eliminated after the company announced it was no longer interested in pursuing that market. Luckily enough, the contract we had developed months earlier provided for a very attractive compensation package. That was because, having repeatedly witnessed firsthand the capriciousness of corporate life, Bob readily adopted the mercenary approach. The irony was that it was Vince who had been give the job of executioner.

The next day Vince called. He was shaken. He had fired people before, but never without any real justification. It was especially painful because of his friendship with Bob. I didn't say, "I told you so." All I said was "Let's talk about your contract tomorrow."

He said, "You mean my condotta."

DON'T IGNORE CHAPTER 5

Even though you may currently have no intention of becoming an entrepreneur, please don't continue further in this book without going back and reading Chapter 5. Mercenaries, even though they're employed, must be somewhat entrepreneurial to maximize their success. Besides, in today's world you're apt to end up on your own, even if only part-time or for a year, while you're changing from one employer to another. That means you'll need to know how to live rich as an entrepreneur.

Living Rich 7

For a philosophy to make the jump from theory into practice there usually needs to be a plan, a systematic application of the principles and attitudes. But the Live Rich philosophy is the exception that proves the rule. There is no prescribed pattern for living rich. In fact, the phrase "Live Rich prescription" is an oxymoron.

While we all want to live rich, that means different things to different people. A rich life is like a fingerprint; no two people have exactly the same one. But at the same time, there's one universal common element to all of our individual visions: freedom.

Living rich means having the freedom to do whatever you want. If I offered a prescribed pattern, a step-by-step application of my philosophy, to you or my clients, I'd be guaranteeing you *wouldn't* live rich. By imposing my plan on you I'd be restraining your freedom rather than empowering you.

While in Part II of this book I'll offer you the Live Rich take on ninety-one individual career and business issues, when, or even whether, you confront them all depends on your own unique situation and circumstances.

In place of offering the "authorized Live Rich plan," let me just briefly go over the concepts once more before you plunge into the specifics of Part II.

To live rich you need to have the freedom to do whatever you want.

In our society it is money that directly or indirectly provides you with the freedom to do whatever you want, to live rich.

For most of us work is the way we obtain money; therefore it's your attitude toward work that will determine whether you live rich.

For your work to help you live rich, you must truly be working for yourself; that means working to meet your own real needs rather than the needs of others or the needs you think you *should* have.

Three axioms or rules can help everyone start to truly work for himself.

The first axiom is: Make money. Your primary reason for working should be to put dollars in your pocket; other goals should be secondary. Work is the only aspect in your life that offers you the chance to make money. Other areas of your life offer better opportunities to pursue those other goals. Look for God in church. Look for satisfaction at home. Look for money at work.

The second axiom is: Don't grow, change. Just as I can't offer you a prescribed plan to live rich, you can no longer rely on following a pre-planned work pattern, whether it's climbing the next rung on an organizational chart or increasing your market share by 10 percent. Look for new opportunities rather than promotions. Look for new markets rather than growing an existing business.

The third axiom is: Take charge. You cannot be reactive and live rich. To become proactive you must stop viewing yourself as a victim and stop letting fear keep you frozen in place. Get out of your own head and out of your own way. Take responsibility for yourself. Stop looking down at the ground for pennies and start looking up in the sky for dollars.

Entrepreneurs and employees each have their own fourth axiom to start truly working for themselves.

The fourth axiom for entrepreneurs is: Create Yourself.com. Your business is nothing more than an avenue for personal profit. Treat it as your child, and you start doing things for it rather than for you. Disown your business and instead create a new personal company, Yourself.com, with the sole purpose of funneling dollars to your wallet. Your current and future businesses are all just temporary ventures for Yourself.com.

The fourth axiom for employees is: Become a mercenary. Your company is not worthy of your unstinting selfless loyalty. You have been a loyal foot soldier for too long. To focus on your own real needs you must become a mercenary, concerned with your income, your professionalism, and your ability to land future work. The only bottom line that should matter is your take-home pay.

I fully realize most of what I'm suggesting is unconventional. Many of my ideas fly in the face of what most people are taught about work. But in my thirty-plus years of consulting with people I've discovered that few of them feel like they're living rich, regardless of how much money they're making or of how much they're serving their community. With so many of them following the conventional advice and so few of them living rich, isn't it time to take a different approach?

I promise you, when you start to truly work for yourself, you'll begin living rich. And this is far more than just a work life transformation. When you realize what your own real work needs are and begin achieving them, you'll feel good about yourself. Your self-image will improve. Your self-confidence will soar.

The Live Rich philosophy offers you a chance at nothing less than freedom and personal empowerment. You will be able to use your earnings to buy the freedom to do whatever it is you want. Just think about that for a minute: finally having the freedom to do what you've always wanted.

Please believe me: The biggest obstacles to your living rich are inside your own head. When you're working for someone else's needs—whether your boss or your parents—you're enslaved. And when you're enslaved it doesn't matter how comfortable those chains are, you're still a slave. You can be earning $500,000 a year, but if you're not truly working for yourself you'll still be living poor. Someone earning $50,000 a year, but working for himself, will be living far richer.

A man physically enslaved by others remains free if his spirit can soar beyond his captivity. But a man who keeps his own dreams locked away will never be free no matter where he goes or what he does. Your mind is the only prison that can ever bind your spirit.*

You can break whatever psychological chains imprison you.

You can fly as high as your dreams will carry you.

You can live rich.

---

*With apologies to Henry Van Dyke, who wrote: "Self is the only prison that can ever bind the soul."

Part II

Putting Theory into Practice

INTRODUCTION TO PART II

The following is an alphabetical examination of ninety-one different topics related to earning money through employment or entrepreneurship. I realize it's far from comprehensive. I've chosen to address only those career and business topics that are approached differently, or that take on an added importance, when you choose to follow the Live Rich philosophy.

None of these chapters is exhaustive. I didn't think this book was the place to go into excruciating detail about, say, financial ratios. That's because you can find that information in any number of good small, business textbooks. Here I'll just explain which I think you should focus on, and why.

Just as in *Die Broke*, I'll be treating these Part II chapters as if they were telephone conversations between you and me. You're a client who has called me and asked, "Stephen, what do you think I should do about my answering machine message?" The chapter is my answer, kept as concise as possible to cut down our time on the telephone and, as a result, your bill.

No one ever calls me and asks, "What do you think about marketing?" That's why, as you've probably already noticed, the chapters are very specific. For instance, there's no "Marketing" chapter, but there are individual chapters on advertising, answering machine messages, answering machines and services, business cards, e-mail, garb and hygiene, gifts, logos, magazine and journal articles, manners and mannerisms, marketing plans, newsletters, press releases, pro bono work and charitable volunteerism, promotional kits, signage, and stationery.

In *Die Broke* I suggested that if there was a personal finance topic I didn't cover in Part II of that book you should turn to the best mainstream advice, which I considered to be *Consumer Reports* and Jane Bryant Quinn's newspaper columns. Unfortunately I haven't yet found any such uniformly excellent sources for guidance on career and business topics. There are lots of good sources out there, but most specialize in one or two areas. As a result, after Part II I've provided a list of some of these sources for further information. If after checking them out you still feel desperate, just give me a call.* We'll talk.

---

*I'm serious. The calls and letters I received about *Die Broke* were both welcome and heartening. The best way to contact me is via e-mail. Send a message to mark4smp@aol.com. If you're not online you can write me via HarperCollins.

Accountants

8

If the only thing a Yourself.com entrepreneur gets out of his accountant is a tax return, then he's wasting his money.

Accountants should serve two general functions for your business: compliance and oversight.

Compliance covers all the regulatory and statutory financial matters a business must deal with. In addition to your personal and corporate tax returns, this includes your sales tax forms and your FICA (Social Security) forms. If he's not a sole practitioner, your accountant can pass this work on to a junior member of the firm and save you some money. If he's not familiar with your particular industry your accountant should be able to learn all he needs to know about regulatory issues by contacting your trade association and speaking with your attorney.

Oversight refers to supervision of your finances. I advise my clients to farm out their payroll, accounts payable, and accounts receivable to an outside firm and concentrate on making money. Your accountant can serve as an excellent check on such outsourced work. To facilitate the oversight, and put the outsourcing firm on notice that it's being watched, I tell my clients to insist that the outsourcing firm send copies of all reports to the accountant too.

Ironically, your accountant can provide at least superficial oversight for outside parties as well, such as investors or bankers who may be lending you money, or someone who may be interested in buying your business. That's why I advise my clients to have their accountant prepare periodic profit and loss statements and balance sheets. Sure, you can generate these reports electronically. But having them prepared by a certified public accountant adds a certain level of integrity to your numbers. You don't need to have the statements certified.* As long as it is his work and the info appears on his stationery that should ordinarily be sufficient.

In addition to compliance and oversight functions, an accountant can serve as a business adviser and a liaison with bankers and other potential lenders.

If you follow my advice and hire an experienced lawyer (see Chapter 51) you can feel free to save some money and hire a young accountant.† Both the oversight and compliance functions require more energy than experience. And if you're using your lawyer for his business wisdom and contacts you won't need an accountant who'll hold your hand or provide introductions.

---

*For a financial statement to be certified, the accountant must physically verify every single number on it. That means he has to scrupulously check your inventory and accounts receivables among everything else. Needless to say, such a process is time-consuming and costly. Banks and suppliers who are extending a considerable amount of credit may require certified financial statements.

†Certified public accountants charge anywhere from $75 to $250 per hour. You should be able to get away with spending less than $5,000 a year for all your business and personal accounting needs.

Advertising 9

You've probably heard the old adage "half of all advertising is wasted, but no one knows how to tell which half." Well, here's the Yourself.com variation on that adage: All advertising is wasted.

Yourself.com businesses are, by their very nature, sharply focused. Advertising, by its very nature, aims for a broad target. The two simply don't match. Advertising is the most expensive and least efficient means of marketing for any Yourself.com business.

Think about how potential customers and clients will find you. If you're a service provider to either businesses or consumers, it will likely be by word of mouth (see Chapter 97), and publicity, not advertising. If you're an Internet or mail order retailer it will probably be by following a series of links, getting a recommendation off Usenet, or using a search engine to find your Web site (see Chapter 96), not via an ad. Even if you're a specialty retailer with a storefront location, it will probably be through your signage (see Chapter 86) and promotion, not because of an ad in the local newspaper.*

Yet most of my entrepreneur clients come to me with marketing plans devoted almost entirely to advertising. I think it's because they

---

*If after carefully studying the question you find that your potential customers or clients *will* find you via an ad, then go for it. After all, it's the exception that proves the rule. For instance, while I wouldn't do it, I think personal injury lawyers are entirely justified in advertising, since that's how many of their potential clients find a lawyer.

think advertising creates an image of substance. Don't get me wrong: Creating that kind of image is vital for a Yourself.com business (see Chapters 12, 13, 18, 25, 32, 39, 40, 53–56, 63, 72–74, 76, 86, 87, 89, and 96). It's just that advertising is the wrong way to go about it. It's expensive and doesn't really convey the image you want. In fact, the only person who's really impressed by a small-business ad is the small-business person himself. Okay, maybe his mother's impressed, too. But that's the extent of it.

Age Discrimination

10

Age is a liability only if you make it so.* That's good news, because as part of the Live Rich (and Die Broke) approach you're going to be looking for new employers and clients throughout your life. You should be going on just as many job interviews or sales calls at age sixty-five as you did at age thirty-five. Therefore, whether you have multiple clients or one exclusive client who calls himself your employer, you need to get them past age and focusing on what really matters: profitability.

In almost every instance of perceived age discrimination, your age isn't the real problem. Instead, the problem is one or more of three common misperceptions in the mind of person with whom you're dealing.

First there's the money issue: The other party sees you as potentially costing more than people who have less experience. He thinks to himself that he can hire someone half your age for half the money. You can either combat that perception or mitigate it.

If you're indeed looking for a salary or fee commensurate with your age, then you must demonstrate why you're a better value, why you're

*I'm writing separately about age discrimination, rather than combining it with other forms of discrimination, because I think it's likely to become the most difficult workplace bias to overcome. I think all other forms of workplace bias are based on nonfinancial rationalizations, and therefore can be defeated by demonstrating a positive impact on the bottom line (see Chapter 50). Ageism, I believe, is based on financial rationalizations that must be directly challenged.

worth the added money. As quickly as possible, show how you, even with your higher salary or fee, can save more money, save more time, or make more money for the other party. On the other hand, you could also choose to accept a lower fee or salary, a figure in line with what a younger person would command. You can easily signal that early in a conversation by saying (whether it's true or not) that your prime concern is enjoying what you're doing, not how much you're getting paid.

No, accepting a lower fee or salary doesn't automatically contradict my earlier advice to focus on making money. If this job or project will enable you to branch out into a new market or industry with longer-term profitability, it could offer value above and beyond the actual dollars. Just don't make a habit of it. And if it's a choice between taking less money for your work or not getting any money at all, there's no question what you should do.

The second issue you need to deal with is being up-to-date. It's wrong, but older individuals are automatically assumed to be behind the times. Just because someone has gray hair doesn't mean she can't surf the Internet. And certainly it doesn't mean she's not on top of the latest developments in her profession or industry. Once again, you need to tackle this misperception as early as possible in your interactions with a potential client or employer. You can do that by both showing and talking about cutting-edge developments in your business. Just make sure that you really are on top of things. There's nothing more pitiful than someone trying to act current who's actually behind the times.

Finally, there's a third age misperception you need to defuse: torpidity. People of every age almost automatically assume that someone older than themselves is less energetic. This is the easiest age myth to shatter. How? By acting young not old. Smile. Laugh. Gesture with your hands. Lean forward in your seat. Show interest and enthusiasm. Every time you laugh or smile you cut five years off your age in the other party's mind. Remember: You're not a tree. You don't have rings around you to clearly mark the number of years you've been on the earth. Age is more a matter of perception and attitude than anything else.

Alliances

11

Yourself.com businesses are, by their very nature, small. To maintain maneuverability and keep profits high they eschew as many fixed assets as possible. That means having as few full-time employees as possible (see Chapter 33), leasing rather than buying equipment (see Chapter 36), and operating out of a briefcase rather than a corner office. But that doesn't mean they also have to entirely forgo taking on major projects or markets: They just need to form alliances.

Business alliances can take as many different forms as there are businesses. They can be very formalized strategic alliances binding two companies to work together on one or more projects. They can also be informal agreements between two individuals to each help augment the expertise, products, or services the other offers.

For instance, in my consulting business I've formed a great many alliances. There's one particular specialist law firm I work with when a client of mine faces litigation. I have alliances with one attorney who specializes in employment law and another whose expertise is patents and copyrights. I'm allied with a number of different accountants, insurance brokers, and financial planners, each with their own unique specializations or skills. There's one particular educational consultant I work with and a number of public relations firms. I even have a working relationship with a personal security firm. All these alliances give me the opportunity to offer my clients services and expertise I couldn't provide on my own.

And like any good alliance, these are reciprocal. Not only do I bring clients to my allies, but they bring clients to me. So in addition to increasing my roster of services, they multiply my marketing reach. They let me take on work I otherwise might not be able to handle.

These kinds of alliances will work for any type of Yourself.com business. A retail operation can form alliances with other noncompetitive retailers who offer complementary products and with firms that repair and maintain products. A copy shop could hook up with a résumé writing service, a desktop publishing person, a Web site designer, a small public relations agency, a freelance writer, and an independent photographer and thus be able to take on a huge variety of printing and publishing projects.

Alliances needn't be between business of similar sizes. A small Yourself.com business could just as well ally itself with a larger more traditional business. There are still benefits for both parties: the Yourself.com business gets added muscle; the larger business gets low-cost access to markets and customers it might not otherwise reach.

You'll need to go out of your way to establish alliances, since most firms and individuals aren't necessarily going to be following the Live Rich program. Be on the lookout for allies in the same places you're scouting for customers: industry functions, professional seminars, trade shows, social events, and community activities. Look for individuals with a skill or expertise you lack that your clients or customers need. Only consider allies who will enhance your reputation. That means they're just as intelligent, well-mannered, attractive, and ethical as you are. Make sure they're predictable. Since you'll be entrusting them with your most precious resources—your customers or clients—you want to be sure of how they'll perform.

The terms of your relationship are best defined by the needs of the client or customer. If the client is looking for convenience or one-stop shopping, or wants you to be their only contact, have your allies bill you. Ask them to give you a wholesale price, since they won't be directly servicing the customer. Then incorporate that price into your own billing. On the other hand, if the client doesn't mind working with multiple contacts you can simply refer him to your ally and let them work out their own financial arrangement. A referral fee could be involved, although personally I'm not a believer in them. As long as referrals go both ways I feel an alliance is innately profitable. After all, it's one of the few ways a Yourself.com can increase business without actually growing.

Answering Machine Messages   **12**

The message on your answering machine or voice mail system is every bit as important to your business's success as your personal appearance, stationery, or Web page. For many potential customers and clients it will be the first impression they have of your business.

Cute messages with background music, children giving the message, or celebrity impressions are annoying for private calls. For a business they're the kiss of death. Your message should be concise, traditional, and clear: Think Jack Webb, not Truman Capote (not that there's anything wrong with Truman Capote).

Ask yourself what information callers would need or want. In many cases, simply stating who you are, that you're unavailable but will return the call as soon as possible, and asking for their name and telephone number is sufficient. On my office's message we add that we're in constant touch with the machine in order to stress and demonstrate our personalized service. Unless you're dealing with customers who have been in suspended animation for a generation you don't need to tell them to wait for the beep. Here's the message on my office's machine:

"You've reached the office of Stephen M. Pollan. No one is here to take your call. However, we're in constant contact with this machine, so if you leave a message we'll get back to you as soon as possible."

If you have a voice mail system offering multiple message boxes and announcements you might want to offer callers a choice. You could ask them to press one to leave a message for you, two to leave a message for your assistant, three to get your mailing address, four to get your fax number, five to get your e-mail address, and six to forward the call to your beeper (see Chapter 67) if it's an emergency. Just make sure the first option you give is to leave a message for you, since that's what most callers will choose.

I'm a firm believer in scripting most business and many personal conversations (see Chapter 84), so I'm certainly in favoring of writing up a script for your answering machine message rather than winging it. And just as scripts require rehearsals, so should the message be practiced a few times before it is recorded.

Give some thought to whose voice you'll use. If you have an assistant or receptionist who normally fields your calls during business hours, it makes sense for the message to be in that voice. In fact, when someone either calls back or is contacted in person, that person will feel reassured to hear the same voice again. That's why the message on my machine is in Anthony's voice rather than my own. On the other hand, if you answer your own telephone your message should also be in your own voice. Having someone else's voice on the message won't fool anyone into thinking you're more than a solo operator. Even if it did, that gullible person would soon start wondering what kind of operation you run if your receptionist is away from her desk at 11 A.M.

Answering Machines and Services   **13**

There have always been a handful of Luddites who argue against answering machines and in favor of answering services. "Some people just hang up when they hear a machine," they say. Or they suggest, "People are more comfortable speaking with another human being." Another favorite argument is "A service can discriminate between those calls that need immediate response and those that can wait."

Well, I can think of only one instance when an answering service makes sense: if you're in a business that requires you to be on twenty-four-hour call. Doctors, veterinarians, even some plumbers, rely on answering services because they need someone who will contact them, regardless of the time, if there's a true emergency. A doctor cannot monitor his answering machine during the middle of the night. A good service will know whether to contact her at home (say a patient has been rushed to the hospital) or to relay the message to another doctor who is "on call" for the evening (little Jimmy can't keep his dinner down).

If you don't need to be available twenty-four hours a day for your customers or clients, an answering machine or voice mail system is fine. Few people other than telephone solicitors hang up nowadays. And any who do will probably just call back later. I think people are actually more comfortable talking to a machine than to people today, especially if they're calling outside of normal business hours. Today when you call an office on the weekend you're expecting a machine; a real person would unnerve you. Finally, there aren't that many services with staff skilled enough to actually make judgments on the urgency of calls. Leaving a message with a bored, insipid, or moronic human is far more frustrating than leaving one on a machine.

Answering machines offer fewer features but cost considerably less than voice mail systems. For most Yourself.com entrepreneurs they should suffice. Simply make sure your machine has the qualities and features you need. Test models before buying so you can hear what outgoing and incoming messages sound like. Digital answering machines, while all the rage, don't necessarily have better sound quality than older tape machines. Look for a unit that's voice activated so clients won't be cut off in the middle of their message. Almost all machines allow for remote retrieval of messages. Better ones will allow remote control of all the unit's functions, even changing messages or turning the machine on and off if need be. Automatic interrupt is a must so you don't find yourself yelling over the message for a client to hold on. Other good features are the ability to record conversations and to give frequent callers a way to skip your greeting and instructions and immediately leave a message.

Before you buy an answering machine, check out the answering services available from your local telephone service provider. Generally this requires you to call in to turn on and/or record your original or new message, and then to call in again to turn off the system and to get your messages. The sound quality of this service is often better than anything you can obtain from a home tape or digital system. The disadvantages are that you won't have as many features as even simple machines, and it's apt to cost you far more over time than even the most sophisticated machines.

If you can afford one, a voice mail system can be an excellent solution for entrepreneurs with complex telecommunications needs. While there are many different types of systems and all sorts of hardware and software configurations, a voice mail system is basically an electronic receptionist. Not only can it direct calls to the right extension or device (telephone, fax, or modem), but it can also take messages for a number of different people or businesses, provide frequently needed information (address, directions, hours, etc.), and seamlessly forward calls to other locations, cellular telephones, or pagers.

It's this kind of savvy use of computer and telecommunications technology that can enable one person not only to do the work of five people, but to run multiple businesses at the same time, and to give the impression of a much bigger operation. Perfect, in other words, for a Yourself.com entrepreneur. There's a catch, of course.

While many of today's personal computers can function as voice mail systems, they can't do so while also serving as your personal computer. It takes a lot of memory to save voice files from messages and image files from faxes. And it takes a lot of processing power to figure out what to do and where to send something. In other words, don't expect your computer to do two jobs at the same time. Usually that means it's your voice mail system when you're out of the office and your computer while you're in the office. So, despite all that fancy technology, if you're alone in the office you're still going to be playing receptionist.

If you need a full-time voice mail system you have three choices.

First, there are simple stand-alone voice mail systems that, while more expensive than telephone answering machines, are far cheaper than complete computer systems. If these fit most if not all your needs, they're a good choice.

Second, you could try to use the voice mail service offered by many local telephone companies. The problem is that while these are cheaper in the short term, they're far more expensive long term. In addition, they may not offer all the features you need.

Third, you could buy a second computer system to serve as your voice mail system. While most expensive in the short term, this option at least guarantees you'll get all the features you need.

Here's a workable compromise that one of my clients came up with: He purchased a stand-alone voice mail machine that serves at least some of his needs. Then, when it came time to replace his computer, rather than trading it in, he turned his old system into a full-time voice mail system.

Automobiles

14

A car is transportation. Period. It's not an investment or an image enhancer. That's why I suggest that my Yourself.com entrepreneur clients lease rather than buy their vehicles, and opt for reliable transportation rather than luxury or performance.

Remember this Yourself.com rule of thumb: Never buy anything you can lease (see Chapter 36). You should certainly not buy anything that depreciates as dramatically in value as an automobile.

Buy a car to fit your needs, not your wants. A Hummer or Rover makes sense only if you are going to be driving up steep muddy trails to visit clients. A normal sports utility vehicle is worthwhile only if you're going to face heavy snows in the winter. And a Boxster is valid only if you'll be flying down the speed-limitless Autobahn between appointments. Otherwise stick with sensible transportation.*

Worried about what your clients or customers will think of your car? Don't be. As long as it's clean, inside and out, they won't think twice. In fact, if you do drive an expensive car they may think you're overcharging.

---

*FYI: I drive a Volvo station wagon because my wife and I carry lots of things back and forth between our apartment in the city and our weekend home in Connecticut, among them, grandchildren. My coauthor drives a Subaru all-wheel-drive station wagon because he has a 150-pound Newfoundland dog and lives in upstate New York's snow belt.

Banking   **15**

I hate to be the one to break it to you, but not only won't banks lend seed money to your Yourself.com business (see Chapter 85), but they probably won't lend it money for working capital either.

Oh sure, they'll tell you all about their small business loan packages and lines of credit for up to $50,000. But take it from me, a former banker, almost every one of those loans and lines of credit will need to be secured by your personal credit. In effect, they'll loan *you* the money, but not your business. That's because if you default they can come after your home and all your other assets.

Even though banks may not be willing to lend money to your Yourself.com business, that doesn't mean they don't want your business, or that you should give them the cold shoulder. In fact, most banks are today going out of their way to land small business customers since that's the fastest-growing segment of their market. And even though they're not willing to express confidence in your business, they can do you some good. Actually, it's not the bank itself that will do you some good, it's a banker.

When choosing a bank for your Yourself.com businesses, insist on getting a personal banker or a specific individual to address your needs. You want someone you can call to expedite transactions, to help smooth applications, to waive annoying charges, and, in general, to make your financial life easier. Your "personal banker" will be a shepherd protecting you and steering you through the bank's red tape and bureaucracy.*

A personal banker may be able to help you get a credit line you could use to even out cash flow problems. He might help you take advantage of the bank's cash management programs so you can earn interest on any extra cash in your business accounts. (Don't laugh, it's possible.)†

Once you find such a personal banker who's willing and able to help you in these ways, make sure you develop a good working relationship with him. Stay in touch with him on a regular basis. Invite him to your parties. Help him get tickets to sporting events and shows. Ask for his advice. Keep him posted on your various projects and opportunities. If he shifts banks, go with him. Making such a move will solidify your relationship and perhaps even take it to the next level. Having moved along with him you'll at the very least gain access to his Rolodex full of contacts and sources. Actually, for a Yourself.com entrepreneur, those additions to your network could end up being more valuable than any short-term small business loan.

---

*Some banks call this approach "core" banking.
†Just one note: Remember you're not in the investment business.

Benefits   16

The only real benefit a Yourself.com entrepreneur needs to offer an employee is a job.

Assume that your employees have all developed the Live Rich attitude. (If they haven't, tell them about it.) That means their primary concern will be to make money, everything else is secondary. It's sufficient for you to offer benefits commensurate with your competitors. If every other small ad agency offers health coverage, offer it to your employees. However, don't go overboard. An HMO is fine, but don't feel you need to cover their families for free or pick up the entire cost of the coverage. If no other small retail shop in your area offers health coverage to employees you don't need to break the pattern.

Sure, offering a better benefits package might attract top candidates. But that's not necessarily your goal (see Chapter 33). You don't want someone working for you who plans on making it his life's work; you may be closing this business in six months and opening another. That means there's no need for you to establish any pension plan, and you certainly don't have to match contributions. I tell my Yourself.com entrepreneur clients to avoid paying for employees' continuing education: It will only result in your losing the person that much sooner.

The only benefits that should matter to mercenary employees are salary and security.

Mercenary employees should opt for getting more money rather than any benefit, since with sufficient money you can buy whatever coverage you need. That being said, health insurance is somewhat attractive. While most individuals could become part of a group that offers coverage, an employer-offered plan will probably cost less. Still, if my client can easily obtain alternative coverage (on his own or through a spouse's policy) I suggest he try to bargain it away.*

Group disability coverage and life insurance are nice, but far from essential. I'd rather you take more home in salary and buy the specific coverage you need. If you pay for your own disability insurance, any payments you receive are tax-free. Pensions are also good, but not critical. You can always set up your own sheltered savings plan. Of course, if you can get an employer to contribute to your pension that's another matter.

One employee benefit I do strongly encourage my mercenary employee clients to push for is payment for their continuing education. Non–Yourself.com employers often thinks it's to their benefit since they're developing a more skilled employee. But the real reason I think it's a good benefit for a mercenary employee is that it's a way for you to speed up your move into another opportunity. Paid education is a way for you to have your employer pick up the cost of your personal marketing.

Finally I suggest my mercenary employee clients be willing to trade in all their benefits for security in the form of an employment contract or termination agreement (see Chapter 35). In a workplace without security the certainty of knowing you're guaranteed a specified income for a specified length of time is likely to far outweigh any doctor bills you'll need to pay.

*Obviously this is a generalization. If there's some unusual medical circumstance that makes finding or carrying your own coverage impossible, my advice would be different.

Bookkeepers and Bookkeeping Software **17**

I have nothing personally against bookkeepers. In fact, some of my best friends are bookkeepers. It's just that I don't think a Yourself.com entrepreneur should hire one.

Bookkeeping is a perfect example of the type of work that today's savvy entrepreneur can replace with technology and outsourcing. Rather than hiring someone to keep your records, pay your bills, collect your receivables, handle your payroll, and keep you in compliance with tax and other regulations, assign the functions to others. One Yourself.com entrepreneur client of mine who runs a small consulting firm was able to pocket over $40,000 more a year by eliminating his full-time bookkeeper, having his accountant handle compliance and oversight (see Chapter 8), an outsourcing firm handle payroll, receivables, and payables (see Chapter 69 and 80) and relying on his computer for record keeping.

The secret to making this kind of system work is to put your accountant in charge. Have her select and set up your bookkeeping software and define the terms of your relationship with the outsourcing company. Asking her to take on this supervisory role may cost you a bit initially, but once the bugs in the system are eliminated, her hourly billings should drop back to normal, and you'll be able to pocket some savings.

While you'll be having your accountant generate periodic financial statements for you (see Chapter 37) you'll want to be able to use your bookkeeping software to get a snapshot look at the health of your business. Ask your accountant to set up the system so you can generate quick profit and loss statements, balance sheets, payables and receivables reports, and cash flow analyses.

Even more important, have the system set up so you can keep a close eye on individual expense categories and how they relate to revenue. That will give you the hands-on control over costs you need to keep your bottom line healthy. Insist on being able to see how much you've spent each month on a particular category; what percentage of monthly revenues that represents; how much you've spent on that category for the entire year until today; what percentage of year-to-date revenues that represents; and how these monthly and year-to-date figures compare with the same numbers for last year.

For example, at the end of the month you call up your delivery costs—say it's $300. You check to see how that compares to your revenue for the month; perhaps you brought in $5,000, meaning delivery costs were equal to 6 percent of your revenue. Then you check the year-to-date figures. You find that in the first six months of the year you've spent $1,000 so far on deliveries and taken in $100,000 in revenue. That means delivery costs have averaged the equivalent of 1 percent of your revenues. Why have your costs gone up for the month? You check the same set of numbers for last year and discover either that this monthly increase is typical and your costs will drop back down next month or that it's an anomaly and merits further investigation.

Business Cards 18

Only one out of every five of my fledgling entrepreneur clients shows up at my office with a serious business plan . . . but they all have business cards. Don't get me wrong. I'm not denying business cards are valuable. In fact, I think they're important for employees as well as entrepreneurs (more on that in a bit). It's just that getting them printed shouldn't be the first thing on an entrepreneur's to-do list.

I think I know the reason for this misguided rush to cards: They serve as a tangible sign of entrepreneurship, a badge you can wear—or at least hand out—that tells everyone you're a businessperson. And since they can be printed inexpensively, they offer a very big psychological bang for your buck.

Despite their allure, I suggest you do yourself a favor and wait before you rush out and either get 5,000 cards printed or run them off on your inkjet printer at home. Instead, give some thought to what you're doing and why.

Just because you can print business cards with your personal computer doesn't mean you should. Homemade cards always look cheap. I don't know why, but while you can get away with homemade return address and mailing labels, I don't think homemade business cards make the grade. Whether it's the traces of perforations around the edges, the canned clip art, the fonts everyone recognizes, the recogniz-ably mass-produced borders, or the less than perfect inking, homemade cards generally say "temporary, inexpensive, and insubstantial." And those are the last three things you want to convey about your business, however true they may be.

The overt purpose of a business card is to provide specific information about you (name, address, telephone number, etc.). The second, more subtle purpose is to provide information about your operation's character. If you want clients to think of you as solid and reliable, your card must convey that by being traditional and conservative in design, typography, and paper quality. Want customers to view you as creative? Then your card should show that.

If you're hiring a designer to create a complete paper package for your business (see Chapter 89), work with the designer to create the right card. If you're not enlisting professional help, turn to a local print shop that has been in business for at least ten years. Someone at that shop will have a working knowledge of what works and what doesn't. Leave the do-it-yourself cards to those who don't know how to live rich. Don't worry—there are plenty of other areas where you can save money without impacting either your image or your performance.

Whether you're an entrepreneur or an employee, if you're following the Live Rich philosophy you should have at least two business cards.

One, obviously, should be from the specific business you're in or the firm that currently employs you. If you're an entrepreneur running more than one business, you should have such a card for each of your operations. Nothing could be worse than finishing off a sales pitch for your new advertising consulting business by handing the potential client a card from your plumbing supply company. You will have undermined everything you've done to demonstrate your seriousness and professionalism.

Your second card should be your personal calling card. For an entrepreneur, this would be the card for Yourself.com. It should give no specific indication as to your business or businesses, simply offering your name and the necessary contact information. This is the card you'll use when you've had a meeting that could involve more than one of your businesses, or that dealt with a new operation so embryonic that cards haven't yet been printed. A personal calling card will go over much better with a potential investor, for instance, than a prematurely printed card for a nonexistent business or a card that implies your attention could be divided.

An employee should have such a personal calling card as well. This can be used in personal and extra-industry networking situations, as well as in situations when you're offering temporary or part-time services while maintaining your current position. The potential client may know you'll be keeping your full-time job while consulting for him on the side. But if you have unaffiliated business cards you'll be implying it's something you do all the time. Your consulting will still be part-time, but it won't be perceived as casual.

Whether you're an employee or an entrepreneur, your personal calling card should have all the simplicity, conservatism, and elegance of a traditional professional's business card. Something like this:

> John H. Hancock
> 1776 Constitution Drive
> Podunk, NY 14856
> Vox: (607) 555-1812
> Fax: (607) 555-1887
> Net: jhancock@clarityconnect.com

While I've never used them myself, I think there might be instances when preprinted Rolodex cards could successfully serve as business cards. All the same rules as for traditional business cards should apply. One drawback, of course, is that you don't know whether a potential client or customer uses a Rolodex, or if he does, what size cards it takes.

A more practical and perhaps just as effective alternative to the traditional card is a three-by-five index card with your contact information printed on top. These can serve multiple roles for you. They allow you to add a personal message if you wish to reinforce a point made at the meeting. They can be used as a replacement for small notecards or postcards. You could use them as a way to add a personalized note to a stack of documents or a more formal letter. Finally, in a pinch they could serve as jotting paper for you.

While both of these alternative offer some interesting marketing opportunities, I don't think they can entirely replace the traditional business card. If you find these useful, I suggest you use them as additional tools, not as replacements for business cards.

I'll discuss other forms of stationery in Chapter 89, but I'd be remiss if I didn't suggest here that you have all your stationery—letterhead, return address labels, and perhaps envelopes—done at the same time, by the same designer and printer. Matching stationery implies consistency and a comprehensive approach to business. If all your business documents look like they've been created at different times, by different people, perhaps for different purposes, it conveys a haphazard approach to operations.

Business Meetings 19

Information technology can be the great equalizer for Yourself.com businesses and mercenary employees. It can enable one person to the work of, and appear to be, five people, and five people to do the work of, and appear to be, fifty people. But there's a potential dark side to all this technology: It can cut down the effectiveness of your one-on-one communications.

You can't beat the convenience or cost of e-mail (see Chapter 32). But it's very difficult to convey shades of meaning and emotions in a written format. That's why those annoying smiley-face characters were invented. (You wouldn't dot the "i" in your signature on a business letter with a little heart, would you? Then don't use those insipid smiley-faces in your business e-mail.) And you certainly can't top the speed of telephone conversations. However, until videophones become common, you won't be able to pick up or send nonverbal messages over the telephone.

Effective business communications, especially the kind of selling and negotiating essential to a Yourself.com company or a mercenary employee, rely on subtlety, subtexts, and emotional messages. Those are conveyed through tone and body language, not necessarily the written or spoken word. It's also much harder to say no in person than it is in writing or over the telephone. Therefore, to increase your chances to live rich you should also maximize your number of face-to-face business meetings.

If you're a Yourself.com business person, you probably won't have the kind of location conducive to such meetings. That means your business meetings will be at the other party's office or a neutral site. However, don't feel as though you've lost the home field advantage. In business meetings there are distinct advantages to being a visitor (for both entrepreneurs and employees). First, by extending yourself and going to the other party's location you demonstrate respect. Second, they'll feel more safe and secure in their own location, so they may be more willing to make immediate decisions. Third, by going to see their place of business you can conduct some surveillance and learn potentially important information about them and their operation. And fourth, as the visitor you can control the speed and duration of the meeting. You're the one who can start off by saying "I have to be back for a three o'clock meeting," or who can call your office to find out there's an unexpected emergency forcing you to cut short a meeting that's not going well.

You can further maximize the effectiveness of your business meetings by controlling their timing, context, and content. The best time is as early in the day as possible since there will be fewer interruptions. Try not to have any important meetings on Mondays or Fridays to avoid postweekend hangovers and preweekend distraction. Always offer to draft the written agenda for a meeting, and make sure it spells out a clear-cut, achievable goal. In every communication about scheduling and confirming the meeting, restate the goal so it sinks in. That way, by the time the meeting takes place everyone involved will at least know the reason they're there.

And that shouldn't be to satiate their hunger.

Everyone who does business with me knows how much I hate business breakfasts, lunches, or dinners. I'm convinced the time and money spent on them is totally wasted. No mentally competent businessperson has ever made a decision based on the fact that you bought him lunch. If you're a Yourself.com business person you're running as tight a ship as possible, so wasting money like that is sinful. For both entrepreneurs and employees, the time spent chatting, ordering, and eating could better be spent working to make more money, freeing up time later in the day for you to spend on your life rather than your work.

Meals out aren't even effective bonuses. If you want to reward staffers or vendors buy them a gift instead. That way the full amount will go to them rather than half of it going to your waistline.

Business/Life Plans

20

Plans are what enable dreams to become real. Without a plan for your business, career, or life, for that matter, you'll never live rich.

I won't take up your time with a lesson on what should go into a business plan. And I won't waste paper and ink reproducing a sample plan that's so generic as to be worthless. There are many excellent books that deal with business plans and that provide boilerplate forms for many different types of businesses. (I've included some of these works in the source list at the end of this book.) However, I do need to make a few points.

As a former banker and venture capitalist I've read thousands of plans, from slick, professionally designed brochures to handwritten notes on a legal pad. The presentation never mattered to me; I looked at the numbers and into the eyes of the entrepreneur. All I needed to know to make a lending or investing decision could be found there. What was the profit potential of the business? What was my exit? Did the entrepreneur have what it took to make the plan real?

Ironically, now that I'm a frequent adviser to businesses, I insist my clients prepare a thorough, comprehensive business plan. That's not because lending and investing decision making has changed; it's because the business plan is essential for the entrepreneur himself.

The act of putting your ideas down on paper forces you to answer questions, to organize your thoughts, and to validate your assumptions. It makes you address difficult issues that are easy to ignore, such as what is the irreducible minimum startup capital and what is the minimum level of sales you need to stay in business.

In effect, the business plan is the gauge by which you can constantly measure your business. Rather than a onetime throwaway promotional piece, I tell my clients that their business plan is a bible. If it has been done honestly, it can be used to predict the success or failure of a new business. And if it's kept up-to-date and modified to fit changing circumstances, it can become a constant measuring stick, an oracle you turn to for guidance each and every day.

It's this quality that makes a business plan essential for your Yourself.com operation. Your goal is to maximize profitability. Your strategy for accomplishing that is to move from one profitable opportunity to another as quickly as possible, abandoning those whose profitability falls below acceptable levels. When you have comprehensive, unbiased business plans drawn up for all your operations you'll be able to quickly see when one of your particular businesses is about to become unprofitable, and immediately shift directions.

The same principle is true for employees who have become mercenaries. That's why I tell my mercenary clients to physically write out a career plan. This plan consists of stated goals, projected timetables, spreadsheets of financial needs and desires, and a complete marketing plan. Every six months I go over the plan with my mercenary clients and we adjust it to fit changes in attitude and measure the clients' current situation against where they wanted to be at that time. I've found that unless employees constantly keep track of their own goals and path they'll unconsciously fall into the trap of working for their employer's needs rather than their own. By taking stock every six months and revisiting your written plan you can quickly decide whether you're still heading in the direction you want to go.

Not only does the principle hold for both entrepreneurs and employees, but I think it should be applied to our personal lives as well as our work lives. While that doesn't mean you need to write up a marketing program for winning a spouse, I do tell my clients to write down their personal goals in a life plan. Where do you want to be living in five, ten, twenty years? What would you like to be doing at each of those stages? What are your long-term goals? What do you need to do financially to achieve those goals and meet those timetables? Are your investments getting you there?

Since I'm not a psychotherapist I don't feel qualified to help people search their psyches to determine what they truly want and need out of life. That being said, I've found that asking my clients to formally draft a life plan often leads to effective self-analysis. Writing a life plan forces you to either plot out ways to turn dreams into concrete goals or to, upon reflection, abandon those dreams as not being what you truly want.

Whether it serves as a tool for self-revelation or not, writing a plan for your business, career, and life forces you to be proactive and makes your goals more achievable. And anything that gets you closer to your own true goals gets you closer to living rich.

Call Forwarding   21

Being able to have your business calls forwarded to wherever you are at any particular time is potentially a great boon to any entrepreneur who is working solo. But it's also a potential disaster.

Calls forwarded directly to you, which are answered in a businesslike manner, will convey an apparently seamless business operation. But if those calls are forwarded to anyone other than you, your business could appear casual, or worse, unsettled. The secret is that there should be no surprises. The caller shouldn't hear anything unexpected when the call is answered.

Just imagine that prospective client you've been trying to reach finally returns your calls, and instead of hearing "John Smith's office" when she's connected, she hears "Reno Motor Inn, short stays our specialty." Sure, after a moment's hesitation she'll ask for you and be connected to your room. But she has been made uneasy. She's troubled. And she's going to be picturing you sitting in the worst no-tell motel her imagination can conjure up, wondering what's going on.

Even a less ambiguous situation is damaging. Perhaps the call is forwarded to your sister's house, where you're visiting for a Memorial Day barbecue. Your fourteen-year-old niece is on the phone with her boyfriend. She gets the call waiting signal and clicks your potential client in. Is she going to field the call in the manner that will help your cause?

There are two solutions. First, use call forwarding only intermit-tently with your own cellular telephone in a way that will ensure all calls will be fielded directly by you at times and places when you can be at your most professional (see Chapter 23). Or second, use call for-warding only as a clearly defined emergency contact system. Have an urgent response mailbox set up on your telephone answering system. Whenever you'll be away change the announcement to say specifically where you'll be, and then offer the individual the opportunity to have the call forwarded. If the client hears a recording of you saying, "I'll be visiting family for the Memorial Day holiday, but can be reached there in an emergency," he won't be shocked or disturbed when your teenage niece fields his call.

Call Waiting

22

It's rare that something can annoy everyone involved in its use. But that's the case with call waiting.

I've heard all the rationalizations. My two favorites are: "Clients don't expect to get a busy signal when they call a place of business," and "It will ensure I don't miss an important call." Actually, clients are more accepting of a busy signal than they are of being interrupted by an obnoxious clicking and then being put on hold. And the only thing call waiting will ensure is that you insult someone.

Let's tackle the busy signal shibboleth first. There are times when every business, no matter how large or how small, will be swamped with telephone calls. A busy signal will more readily be interpreted as a sign that you're successful rather than as an indication you're underequipped. It's certainly far less annoying than having a robotic voice tell you all lines are busy and being put on hold, or to have your important call interrupted by another call. If it's apparent one voice-dedicated telephone line isn't enough for your business, simply add a second unlisted number. Have your answering system set up so that when your primary voice line is busy, incoming calls are bounced to your unlisted second line, and are answered by the machine after three rings or less.

Now let's discuss the missing call myth. Few business deals have ever been lost because of busy signals. If you're looking for reflexive telephone business, just make sure you have the biggest, boldest ad in the Yellow Pages and that your company name starts with AAA. If that's not your main source of business, don't worry about a customer getting a busy signal now and then. He'll call back. Don't you? Even if you do miss one deal, it's better than the alternative: having to show a client or customer that he's not your top priority.

Call waiting forces you to openly make choices, to clearly prioritize your callers. Whenever I'm with a client in person or talking to one on the telephone, I tell him and show him that he is my number one priority. How do you feel when you're on the telephone with someone, hear those clicks, are asked to hold, and then are told the party has to take the other call? If it's a personal call and the new message is your friend's son calling from the hospital, you understand. If it's a business call and you're the one soliciting business, you get annoyed but accept it. If it's a business call with someone you're paying and she takes another call, you get livid. You hang up, think "Now I know how unimportant my business is to her," and start looking for a replacement.

If you have teenagers at home and get them to swear to always click in new callers and take messages, call waiting can make sense for a family. But for a business it does more harm than good.

Cellular Telephones **23**

I'm as attached to the telephone as anyone. At about 8 A.M. almost every weekday morning I'm on the telephone with my coauthor, Mark Levine. From then until about 7 P.M. I'm probably on the telephone at least thirty minutes out of every hour. On the weekends I'll usually have one or two business calls each day. When my family and I spend two weeks on Martha's Vineyard during the summer I'm working the telephones at least three hours a day. The only time I'm out of touch with either my office or its answering machine for more than four hours is when I'm sleeping or on an overseas vacation. And yet I don't use a cellular telephone.

I've found that if I have at least one competent person in my office during normal business hours, a decent telephone answering device with remote access capabilities turned on during nonbusiness hours, and adequate access to a public telephone—whether on the side of the road, at an airport, in an airplane, or at a client's office—I don't need to carry a telephone with me everywhere I go. I simply make sure to check with Anthony at my office or with my answering machine on a regular basis. And if there's an emergency, Anthony can always patch me into a call wherever I am. The basic charges and per call fees for cellular telephone service make it too expensive to be simply an ego booster or status symbol.

I'm able to get by without a cellular telephone because I have

Anthony back at the office fielding my calls. If your business involves personal service and/or tight deadlines and you don't have someone like Anthony in your office, or you're often in situations where public telephones aren't readily accessible—perhaps you spend a lot of time driving the interstate—then you need a cellular telephone.

The best system for integrating a cellular telephone into your daily business is to couple it with an answering machine (see Chapter 13) and call forwarding (see Chapter 21), both of which you can activate and deactivate quickly and easily. When you're out of the office and will be able to receive calls—say you're on the train traveling home or on the road between appointments—your call forwarding should be active, transferring calls to your cellular telephone from your business line. But as soon as you get home, arrive at a client's office, or are in any other situation when you don't want to be disturbed by calls, you shut off your call forwarding and activate your answering machine. When you finish up at the client's office you turn off the answering machine and reactivate the call forwarding. And when you get back to the office you turn them both off. With this kind of system you can be accessible to clients as often as possible without having an Anthony to field your calls.

Two final notes: First, try to limit your cellular telephone use to fielding incoming calls. Wait until you can get back to your office or to a public telephone to make your outgoing calls. You'll save substantially. And second, if you do opt for a cellular telephone, please don't use it while driving, walking down the street, or attending an entertainment event. Not only is it dangerous and rude, but it's unprofessional. When you're speaking with a client on your cellular telephone he shouldn't be able to tell you're not sitting at your office. That means you should answer it in the same manner and with the same greeting as you do your office telephone. And that also means he shouldn't hear any street noise, car horns, or audience laughs in the background.

Child Care Issues

When people ask me how to raise wonderful, successful children like my four kids I honestly say I don't know, and give them my wife's telephone number.

Seriously, I wasn't there, physically or emotionally, for most of their childhoods. I was at the office from dawn to dusk, and even when I got home I was mentally still on the job. While I've tried to make up for my shortcomings during the past few years, that makes me the least likely person to offer advice on child rearing.

But it also makes me the best person to offer advice on the costs of having someone else raise your children. Everyone, even I, know that good child care is tough to find and expensive. My advice is to focus on the true costs of child care, and how it affects your efforts to live rich.

Do not automatically assume it makes economic sense for both parents to continue working. If both parents are earning large salaries it probably does. But if both salaries aren't big ones it may not.

When you add the cost of child care to the litany of expenses involved in working (clothing, cleaning, commutation, entertainment, etc.) you may find almost all of one of those dual incomes is being spent. Factor in the emotional and psychological toll of one parent not being with the child, and the nonwork time that must be devoted to mundane tasks (cooking, cleaning, shopping) rather than activities with the child, and you may find it doesn't make sense for both parents to go back to work.

There are, of course, compromise positions. While it wouldn't be easy for the first couple of years, the stay-at-home parent could start a full- or part-time home-based business, find a telecommuting position, or work out a flextime arrangement if he feels the need to keep a foot in the workplace.

I suppose all I'm really suggesting is that when it comes time to choose between staying home with a child and going back to work you truly consider which would make your life richer. One of the things money can't buy you is time with your young children. Believe me. I know.

Client and Customer Relations **25**

Good client and customer relations are important for every employee or entrepreneur. But they're essential for those who intend to live rich. Without a large organization or staff to back her up, a Yourself.com entrepreneur is probably, for better or worse, the only face a client or customer will ever see. Similarly, a mercenary employee, moving from one opportunity to another, must be able to forge and maintain his own solid client or customer relations, totally independent of a particular employer or company. I realize that's quite a burden. However, I've discovered three secrets. The first is: The key to good client and customer relations is trust.

With so many skilled people around, and with so much regulation and accreditation, most clients and customers can quickly determine whether a person or business has the skill or product that fits their needs. What they can't readily determine is your character. Will you do your best for them? Will their interests be your priority? In effect, can they trust you?

It takes time for trust to develop naturally in a relationship. The client or customer, over the course of working with you for months or years, can gain ample firsthand evidence of your trustworthiness. But if you're trying to live rich you're not going to have that kind of time; you may be in an entirely new business or with a different company in a year. That's where my second secret comes in: The shortcut to trust is caring.

When a client or customer senses you care for him as an individual human being, he trusts you. That means your customer/client relations program should consist of demonstrating, every day and in every way, how much you care.

How you do that depends, to some extent, on your specific situation. What works in a personal service business may seem out of place, even outlandish, in a retail operation. With that caveat in mind, let me tell you my third secret: The best time to show a client or customer you care is your first business meeting with him.

Once you've been selected by a client or customer, stop trying to sell him. When a client comes to see you or you go to see him, spend your time demonstrating how much you care, not why you should be hired. Assume if they're in your office or store, or you're in theirs by invitation, they've already made their choice and you're it. The best thing you can do is create trust. Do it right and even if the client wasn't already sold, he will be by the end of the meeting.

One of my retailer clients is a master at creating trust between her staff and her customers. She makes sure her salespeople aren't chewing gum, smoking, eating, or having extended conversations on the telephone while a customer walks around the store. Instead, she insists that every customer be acknowledged with a smile, a pleasant greeting— "Good morning/afternoon/evening" is sufficient—and a statement that the salesperson is available if the customer has any questions or needs any help. Then the salespeople give the customers space, yet remain aware of them, looking for signals they need help. In effect, they act like a very good waiter who magically appears just when you need him. Such an approach shows customers that the store cares enough to acknowledge customers, offer assistance, and then give them the privacy they need.

In a personal service business, things are little different. As soon as a client, new or established, comes to my office, one of my staff greets him by name, takes his coat and umbrella, directs him to a seat, asks if he'd like coffee or a glass of water, and asks if he'd like to use the bathroom. When all that's accomplished the staff member says, "Stephen is on the telephone, but he'll be out to see you in just a moment." I specifically instruct my staff to refer to me as Stephen, rather than as Mr. Pollan, in an effort to make as a quick a personal connection as possible.

While waiting in the outer office the client can browse my bookshelves, or just sit and listen to the soft classical instrumental music that's playing constantly. He can see my staff, all dressed in traditional office garb (there's no dress-down day in my office—see Chapter 40), working hard at their desks (staff members are not allowed to eat at their desks). I believe that when a client sees a staff that looks and acts informally, the client consciously or subconsciously will think the business isn't giving its clients 100 percent.

When I come out to greet the client I'm always wearing my jacket. I smile broadly, shake hands, and subtly bow at the waist to reinforce that I'm working for him. I tell him to call me Stephen and then again ask if he'd like coffee or water or would like to use the bathroom. I know he's already been asked those questions, but my repeating them really reinforces the message that everyone in this office cares about him.

Before entering my private office, and within the client's hearing, I tell my staff not to disturb me unless it's an emergency. They know this is standard operating procedure, but I state it out loud nevertheless so the client can hear it. This shows again how much I care. It also provides an immediate rationalization for any interruption that does occur.

Once inside my private office I guide the client to a seat. I then ask what I can do for him. During the conversation I make sure to tell the client exactly what my office will do and who will be doing it. If any work will be delegated to someone outside the office I get him on the telephone to make a quick introduction (see Chapter 26). If work will be done by a staff person I call him into the office for an introduction. I think going out of the way to make such introductions shows I care for the client's comfort above all else.

I always bring up costs. That way the client doesn't fell uncomfortable asking (and also won't feel the urge to negotiate). I tell him what the work is likely to cost (I charge by the hour but provide an estimated total, or budget), and explain what circumstances could cause that cost to increase (such as inefficiency of the other side). I stress that he'll be told of any potential increased cost as early as possible. I repeatedly tell him that everything will work out well. I stress that I'm available outside of normal business hours if he needs me, yet again demonstrating how much I care. (I also make a point of immediately returning the first of any such out-of-business-hours calls I get.)

If appropriate, I give him something to go home with. It could be a copy of one of my books or articles that are relevant. It might be the pad I gave him to take notes in the office. Maybe it's a recommendation of a restaurant up the street where he should have lunch. Or it could just be calling downstairs for the doorman to hail a cab for him. Whatever it is, this kind of gesture not only shows I care, but mentally extends his visit to my office.

Finally, as he's about to leave I thank him for hiring me, reinforcing that I'm working for him, and yes, that I truly care about him.

Whenever I explain this approach to customer and client relations, some people get uncomfortable. They think I'm advising insincerity. Far from it. I DO care about my clients. Without them I can't live rich. They are vital to me. The same should hold for you and you clients and customers. Without them you're out of business. All I'm doing is everything I can within reason to demonstrate how much I care. It's not different from saying hello, thank you, you're welcome, or have a nice day. It's not insincerity: It's politeness. It's also smart business.

Conference Calls 26

Conference calls are sometimes a necessary evil.

Face-to-face meetings are better than any telephone call (see Chapter 19). And a telephone call involving more than one person is even less effective than a one-on-one conversation. The dynamics are far different. Rather than a give-and-take or back-and-forth, conference calls are, at best, ineffective searches for consensus, and at worst, filibusters. That being said, they do have a role in your Live Rich plan.

People who are used to working together as a team can often use conference calls as substitutes for staff meetings. However, as soon as outside parties are brought in, discussions should take place in person.

Any time you need the speedy concurrence of more than one person in a situation close to conclusion, you can place a conference call. Not only will you save time and money, but you can use peer pressure to help get you the answer you want.

Finally, when you need to make people who aren't interacting directly aware of each other, you can introduce them via a conference call. I often use this technique when I'm bringing in a professional ally (see Chapter 11) to work on a client's project. I place a call to the client, tell him about my plan, and then patch the allied professional into the call. He then offers some words of reassurance to the client. The client feels better knowing his fate is in the hands of a real person, not some voiceless abstraction.

Continuing Education   27

If you want to live rich you can't rely on the passage of time or your own reading to become smarter; you must proactively go out there and take classes.

Whether you're a mercenary or a Yourself.com you must constantly be expanding your skill base and knowledge. More skills means access to more markets for yourself or your businesses. Furthering your education at a university, industry seminar, or a respected formal personal development program (such as Toastmasters) can become part of your self-marketing and promotion. For instance, both employers and clients might be impressed to find out you're learning to speak German. Education adds to your networking possibilities. You could make good contacts among your fellow students, but more important, teachers or professors can often serve as excellent networking bridges into other industries, fields, or disciplines.

What should you study? Courses in business disciplines such as finance, marketing, and management are good choices for mercenaries if they broaden your expertise. Classes in professional areas such as law, accounting, and insurance can help Yourself.com entrepreneurs both in running their businesses and in servicing their clients or customers. Finally, classes in basic communication skills such as foreign languages, writing, and public speaking can help anyone and everyone.

Corporations

28

Every Yourself.com business should be incorporated.

First, while you'll be paying your accountant more, since he'll be preparing two returns (personal and corporate), there are some distinct tax advantages to incorporation. The government seems less likely to audit a corporate return than a personal return reporting the same numbers.

One of the "audit flags" on a personal return is Schedule C income.* There's no Schedule C on a corporate tax return, yet the same income and expenses can appear on it with less fear of an audit. In fact, the government rarely audits small corporations. Apparently there's a perception that an individual is more likely to "cook the books" than is a corporation.

"C" corporations—other than those engaged in "personal services"—can pay lower overall taxes by keeping some of profit to be taxed at the low 15 percent federal corporate tax rate. At the time this book was written medical insurance premiums were fully deductible for a "C" corporation, but only partly deductible for an "S" corporation or sole proprietor.†

---

*Schedule C is the form attached to a return that explains a sole proprietor's self-employment income and expenses.

†"C" and "S" are simply two different forms of incorporation. They each have distinct advantages and disadvantages. Your accountant can help you select the structure best for you.

Second, corporations offer liability protection. If you're incorporated, only corporate assets can be attacked in a suit against your business. Your personal assets are shielded provided you don't mix them with business assets and you keep up-to-date corporate minutes. For most sole practitioners or independent businesses this added protection is a good idea. For a Yourself.com entrepreneur it's a must. That's because you're apt to be involved in multiple businesses at the same time, dramatically increasing your liability exposure.* Ask your attorney about the advantages and costs. Once again, she'll be happy to talk to you about incorporation since she'll be able to charge you for filing the paperwork.

Third, and most important, being incorporated adds the appearance of substance to a Yourself.com business. Even though almost everyone knows how easy it is to incorporate, there's still magic to having those initials "Inc." or "P.C."† after your business's name. Corporations are perceived as being larger, more established, more predictable, and more substantial than any other form of business. You'll be spending thousands of dollars in other areas of your business to try to create just the kind of image you automatically get from spending a couple of hundred dollars and becoming a corporation.

There are new alternatives to incorporating that are available in most states. The most popular are the limited liability company (LLC) and limited liability partnership (LLP). While these forms give you some of the same protections as corporations, you need to speak with your professionals and explore whether they work for you. For what it's worth, neither yet offers the prestige of incorporation.

Every state has different rules and regulations about incorporating. There are how-to books that provide preprinted forms, and there are services that will help you prepare and file the paperwork. These do-it-yourself and do-it-cheap methods are theoretically sufficient for setting up simple corporations with one class of stock. But just as I don't encourage people to use tax preparation services, I'd rather you didn't use these methods. This is serious business. Hire an experienced lawyer and make sure it's done right. It will cost you a bit more, but it's money well spent.

---

*Incorporating doesn't eliminate the need for professional malpractice or errors and omissions insurance. The "corporate veil" can often be pierced in cases of negligence.
†P.C. stands for personal corporation. My business, for instance, is Stephen M. Pollan, P.C.

Creditor Relations

29

If you're a Yourself.com entrepreneur it's safe to assume banks aren't going to be knocking down your door offering your business money.

Whatever credit you get from a bank is probably going to come in the form of personally guaranteed loans or credit cards. Since banks aren't willing to treat you as a "partner," you should keep them at arm's length as well. That means showing them no loyalty. (If you have an excellent relationship with a "personal banker" you can show *him* loyalty.) Take advantage of every break you can. If you see a lower rate or better deal offered by another bank, ask your bank to match it. If it refuses, shift your business. Banks are so competitive and the application process is so painless that I see no reason why a Yourself.com shouldn't become a serial debtor, moving from bank to bank whenever there's an opportunity to save a dollar or two (or whenever your "personal banker" shifts employment). The only time I'd suggest you show loyalty to a bank is if it recognizes your business as being "bankable" on its own.

Your best source of business credit is apt to be your suppliers. They are automatically your partners, and all it takes to turn them into ready creditors as well is to actually treat them like partners. Ask them for advice about the industry in general and your business in particular. Explain how you talk them up to everyone you meet, stressing how you're not only a customer but a marketing tool for them as well. Flatter them shamelessly. Give them all the credit for your successes and take the blame for all their failures. Invite them to your daughter's wedding and your son's bar mitzvah. Then, during the cocktail hour, ask about extended terms, deferred payment plans, consignment programs, and any other devices they offer that can help your cash flow.

Delivery Services

30

Yourself.com entrepreneurs shouldn't form foolish loyalties. Just because Fed Ex sent you free tracking software, or your UPS driver is friendly, that's no reason to use either of them as opposed to, say, the U.S. Postal Service.

Each of the major delivery services has its own unique advantages. The secret is to maintain accounts with each and select the right service for your particular needs at the moment. Need a document to be delivered first thing the next morning? Perhaps Fed Ex makes the most sense. Need a larger box shipped in a couple of days? UPS might be the most affordable. Have a document you need to arrive in two to three days and you aren't concerned with tracking it? The Postal Service could be the most efficient and economical.

Don't fall victim to false convenience either. Pickups are easy to arrange and your letter carrier is at your office and home once a day. There are mailboxes and drop boxes everywhere today if you stop to look. And look twice. There may be just a Fed Ex drop box inside your neighborhood Kinko's. But I'll bet there's a UPS drop box and a U.S. Postal Service mailbox right outside the store.

Another option is to pass along package delivery costs to clients or customers. While it's accepted practice in most retail businesses, more than a few service providers are hesitant to pass along such charges. However, if you make it clear from your first meeting that you'll be billing for out-of-pocket costs (photocopying, faxing, delivery), then I see nothing wrong with it.

Finally, regardless of who's paying the bills, use e-mail (see Chapter 32) whenever possible for document transmittal. It's always the fastest, cheapest, and most environmentally sound method, and often it's the most convenient too.

Discrimination

31

Yourself.com entrepreneurs should see only one color: green.

Race, religion, gender, disability, sexual preference, and national origin are meaningless. (See Chapter 10 for my feelings on age discrimination.) All that counts is profitability. Whoever does the work in the manner that's most profitable to you is the best person for the job. In fact, the Live Rich philosophy transcends even species barriers: If a machine or animal does the job more profitably than a person, it should get the job. Discriminate on the basis of anything other than profitability and you're not going to be living rich.

Admittedly, not every employer will follow this philosophy. Mercenary employees may well have to face suspected discrimination. I think there's only one way to deal with it. Make the best case you can that you're the candidate who will add more to company's bottom line than anyone else. If that's not enough to overcome an employer's prejudices, then it's not the kind of place you should be working. Any business that still places personal prejudice above profitability is bound for bankruptcy. I guess there is some justice in the world after all.

E-Mail

32

E-mail is too easy. Because you can simply click reply and in a few seconds type a response to a message, that's what most of us do. When the original note was a message from your buddy on the other side of the globe or your sister across town, that's fine. But when it's a note from a business client it's problematic.

E-mail is chronically unpolished and informal. It is usually riddled with spelling mistakes, sometimes filled with shorthand abbreviations, and occasionally littered with inane smiley faces. All this is fine for personal exchanges, whether among colleagues or friends, but not for communiqués with current or future clients or customers.

On the other hand, e-mail is the perfect communication medium for those who want to live rich. It offers speed, affordability, and flexibility. An e-mail sent to Afghanistan takes no longer and costs no more than one sent crosstown. And that message can be sent or received wherever and whenever you can use a laptop computer or electronic organizer. E-mail is now, and will continue to be, the communication method of choice for most small-business people.

What's needed, then, is to add an element of thoughtfulness to what's now a reflexive process. Your e-mail messages to clients and customers should be considered and crafted with the same care you give to written correspondence, and the same care I urge you to give to verbal communications (see Chapter 84 on scripting). While you can't control the entire appearance of your message (those preferences are determined by the recipient's software settings), you can control enough to make sure your messages look and read like professional communication. And while you can't dictate the circumstances behind the e-mail communications you receive, you can dictate how and when you send e-mail. Here are some suggestions.

Spell-check every message you send to a client or customer. If your e-mail application doesn't allow you to check spelling, either buy one that does or pick up an add-on spell-checking utility.

If you feel it necessary to "quote" the message you're responding to, do so at the end of your own message. For hundreds of years it has been sufficient to simply say, "in response to your letter of April 7, regarding the sale of widgets to Acme Inc. . . . " Just because you can now insert comments into the original text of a message and then resend it doesn't mean you should. Think first of how you'd respond if you'd received the original message on paper. If you'd have simply jotted your comments in the margins and returned the original, it's okay to insert additions into quoted text. If, on the other hand, you'd have written a new message on a separate piece of paper, don't insert comments into quoted text.

Don't bother indenting paragraphs, since every application seems to treat tab stops differently. Instead, start every paragraph flush left and simply leave one line of white space between each paragraph. That will clearly define your paragraphs whatever your recipient's application or settings.

Letterheads and dates are unnecessary; however, make sure you use a formal, informative "signature" at the end of your documents. Avoid favorite quotations and clever graphics composed of dashes or letters on your business messages. Instead, provide your name, title, company name, address, telephone numbers, and e-mail address at the end of every message.

Respond to e-mail messages as soon as possible. E-mail is, or at least should be, used primarily for speed. The sender has indicated the need for a quick response by selecting e-mail rather than sending a fax or a letter. You should meet this need. If you can't offer a complete answer send a note of acknowledgment, promising to get back to him as soon as possible.

Remember you can also respond by telephone. Phone calls are just as quick as e-mail (if not quicker) and almost always result in clearer understanding between the parties. (The exception is conference calls.) Just because you received an e-mail message doesn't mean you can't respond with a telephone call. If you can offer yes or no answers to questions, or ask questions that only need such straightforward responses, e-mail is fine. If the questions or answers are more subtle and may need some back-and-forth discussion, pick up the telephone instead. Going back and forth via e-mail multiple times won't save any time or effort.

Always double check you're not sending your note to people you don't wish to see your response. Many people routinely send copies of their e-mail messages to superiors, subordinates, and/or interested parties. If you simply give the reply command you may be sending a note back to all those individuals.

Don't send jokes or chain letters, no matter how funny or worthy, to business contacts. If you get a great Monica Lewinsky limerick via e-mail and have an uncontrollable urge to pass it along, send it to your friends, not your clients.

Never send or respond to "spam" (unsolicited e-mail offers). Sending indiscriminate solicitations brands you as a shyster. Responding, even if it is allegedly to get you off the list, will just guarantee you get more. Instead, add the address to a list of senders your application will automatically filter out.

Employees

As a Yourself.com entrepreneur you've developed an entirely new approach to your business to finally live rich. If you're going to have any employees, you need to develop an entirely new approach to them as well if you want to live rich.

First, and most important, have as few employees as you possibly can. Every employee you have directly reduces your personal profits. If you can possibly maintain and present your business in a professional manner without any employees, go it alone. If you can replace people with machines, do it. It costs less money to buy a sophisticated computer system and continually upgrade it than it does to find and pay a decent administrative assistant. If you need occasional help for specific tasks, either farm the work out to another Yourself.com business (see Chapter 66 on outsourcing and Chapter 44 on independent contractors) or hire a temp (see Chapter 92).

Since you'll be emphasizing change and flexibility in your business, and you'll be employing as few people as possible, you shouldn't be looking for someone to fill a specific job—it could vanish the first time you switch businesses or directions. Instead, look for someone to do a certain kind of work that will need doing regardless of what specific business you're in. For instance, if you'll be having clients come to your office, you may always need a receptionist, regardless of why those clients are coming to see you. That means skills and flexibility are probably more important than specific experience.

Because there will be so much change in your business you need whatever staffers you *do* have to be predictable. Their ability to do the work you give them at a certain proficiency should be a given, since little else will be. For a Yourself.com entrepreneur it's better to have an employee who does steady B-level work, rather than someone who sometimes does A work but other times does C work. Look for someone who'll come in at 9 A.M. every day rather than someone who'll come in late three times, and then early two times to compensate.

Intelligence is always good, but I suggest Yourself.com entrepreneurs place an even higher priority on candor and humility. Sometimes very intelligent individuals have a hard time admitting they don't understand something, don't know how to do something, or made a mistake It's better to have employees who are humble enough to ask for help when they need it than rocket scientists who won't admit they're in over their heads. The former may not hit as many home runs, but they'll make fewer errors. And that's more important. You're the power hitter in this business. As a Yourself.com entrepreneur you want the game riding on your performance alone. Look for B-level people with candor, rather than A-level people.

Your expectation should be that someone will stay with you for one to three years. Any less and you'd be better off with a temp. Any more and you'd be better off outsourcing the job or working with an independent contractor.

Besides giving priority to different traits, Yourself.com entrepreneurs need to redefine the employer/employee relationship. This new relationship can be summed up in one simple word: honest.

You need to assume your employees will have read this book, too. They'll be mercenaries. Rather than looking to you to provide them with long-term security, they'll have one eye focused on their work for you and another looking out for their next opportunity. That's okay, since you'll have one eye focused on their work and the other on your own personal bottom line. The moment that bottom line starts to head into the red you'll be drafting their pink slip. As long as you both understand this new relationship, and neither of you expects any more from it, you should each be happy.

To ensure this level of understanding, have a direct, open conversation with every one of your new hires, telling them their continued employment depends on your profitability as well as their performance, and saying you understand that they need to be constantly looking for new opportunities.

You may even want to discuss a termination package in advance. This won't jinx the relationship from the start: That's already been done by forces beyond the control of both of you. As surely as the sun rises and sets you will be terminating them or they will be leaving you. Admit the inevitable and prepare for it and you'll both be better off.

If you're lucky enough to have a self-starter on your staff, consider making him a partner rather than giving him a raise. Since you'll be looking to change and shift your own direction, a truly self-sufficient employee could be given charge of a business or product line that you otherwise would abandon. The traditional reward for management duties is a salary increase. But in your case that would serve only to lower your personal profitability and perhaps kill the business. Instead, offer a healthy share of the profits. Since his salary is staying the same your expenses won't increase. He'll be motivated to boost the business to increase his own personal profitability. And while your take from this specific operation may not grow, you'll certainly have a better chance of maintaining. After all, the alternative to giving an employee equity could be just to kill the business, and that's going to eliminate all your profits from it.

Employment Agencies 34

I've become a big fan of employment agencies for both my mercenary employee clients and my Yourself.com clients.

From both the entrepreneur's and the employee's perspective, an employment agency saves a great deal of time and increases your chances of finding a situation that's a good match.

Every entrepreneur will tell you one of his most daunting tasks is finding good people. So why not hire someone whose profession is finding good people? A good agency is better at checking references, gauging skills, and determining personality than any entrepreneur could be. I've found that rather than having to interview ten people to come up with two good candidates, when an employment agency is used you interview four people who are all good candidates. In other words, you spend less time on the task and get better results. That's great for any entrepreneur, but it's particularly valuable for a Yourself.com entrepreneur who will be doing more himself and who places a higher priority on speed.

Similarly, every job hunter will complain of having to interview for five jobs that aren't right for every one that is right. And then there are the "going through the motions" interviews: situations when someone has already been selected but the employer, for legal or political reasons, has to make a show of recruiting. A mercenary employee who works through an employment agency goes on fewer total interviews, but they're each good potential matches. Once again, you'll spend less time and get better results.

So what's the catch? Simple. Money. Employment agencies charge either the employee or the employer. Some even charge both. A fee of 10 percent of the annual salary is fairly common. I don't think that's an unreasonable charge for the time savings and improved results. However, I have a big problem with either my employee or my entrepreneur clients paying this in a lump sum.

As a Yourself.com entrepreneur you'll be focusing on change rather than growth, and also doing everything you can to minimize your staff. That means you may not even want to have this person on the payroll for the whole year. And if you're a mercenary employee you may not even want to be on the payroll for the whole year. After all, you'll be using your bifocal vision to constantly look for new and better opportunities.

The solution for both employees and entrepreneurs is to negotiate a payment plan. Rather than paying in a lump sum, divide the total fee by twelve and turn it into a monthly payment. If the relationship lasts you'll end up paying the same fee. But if it doesn't for whatever reason, you won't have suffered out-of-pocket damage. Don't fall for talk of agency "guarantees." They're useless. All they'll do is require you to use the same agency that's just failed you.

Employment Contracts 35

The two most important elements of a job to a mercenary employee are stream of income and security. You can maximize your stream of income by focusing on making money as your primary work motivation. And in today's environment, the way to maximize your security is to get an employment contract.

Surprisingly, most employment contracts today are actually initiated by employers. Often they result from the company being up for sale or part of a merger negotiation. For the company to guarantee to a potential buyer or partner that its key personnel are kept in place, it tries to sign important employees to contracts. In other instances, the company starts the process by asking employees to sign secrecy or noncompete agreements. Savvy employees, realizing these are just one-sided employment contracts, negotiate an expansion of these documents into broader agreements, at least covering termination and severance issues.

Of course employees can initiate contract negotiations, but that's much more difficult. My clients who have been successful at this have used three techniques: turning a raise discussion into a contract negotiation; soliciting an outside offer that includes a contract, and using that as leverage to get a contract from the current employer; or asking for a termination agreement, which serves the same basic purpose (you know you'll be getting x dollars for x years), instead.

There's no boilerplate employment contract, so everything in it—

from compensation to termination—is open to negotiation. There's also no standard of fairness. This is the ultimate in workplace free agency. As an employee you're entitled to whatever you can get, just as an employer is entitled to whatever he can get.

Even though one of your new maxims is to focus on change rather than growth, don't shy away from a long-term employment contract of, say, three to five years. Despite what the employer and his lawyers may think, there's really very little a company can do to keep you from working someplace else. Courts have generally ruled that companies cannot keep you from either quitting or making a living. They may be able to keep you from working in a specific geographic area or for certain competitors for a short period of time (through noncompete agreements and negative covenants), but the broader the restrictions they place on you, the less likely the agreement is to stand up in court. Just to be safe, however, you may want to negotiate a provision that allows you to give notice to quit for good reason.

Even though the most heinous restrictions are hard to enforce, it's a mistake just to ignore these secrecy provisions and negative covenants. Your employer will require they be in a contract and so you need to be wary of the restrictions they do place on you. Try to limit the time of restrictions to one year or less and to narrow the geographical limits to which you're subject.

Make sure your function is clearly spelled out. While a job title is important to determine your position in the hierarchy of the company, it may not fully describe your duties. Your primary duties and the individual to whom you report should be stated. This makes what you're supposed to do, and whom you need to answer to, very clear, avoiding "unofficial" demotions. (You could still be called vice president, but be told you have to mop the floors.) Your contract should also state that if there's a significant change in your job description, you have the right to terminate the contract and receive payment for the remainder of its term or for your agreed severance payment, just as if the company terminated you "without cause."

Employment contracts should include specific language about your compensation, clearly stating your annual salary, how often you will be paid, what deductions will be made from your salary, and what bonuses, if any, you may be due. It should say that your salary will be reviewed at least once a year during your tenure. This gives you an opportunity to push for performance-based pay increases.

If your salary or bonuses are tied to profitability or performance, the formulas for determining those amounts should be spelled out. If you'll be receiving regular cost-of-living increases, those should also be described. The same goes for stock options.

You should also consider asking for a signing bonus or, if applicable, a "staying" bonus. This is money that's yours no matter what happens. Large employers today want to recruit and retain the best and are often willing to pay for it.

Every other perquisite or benefit you receive must also be included in the contract. You may feel funny about having your agreement get into vacation days and insurance coverage details, but if those aren't included the company doesn't have to give them to you. I've seen companies use the lack of specific language about issues both parties thought were "understood" as leverage against employees.*

Try to get a minimum number of weeks' or months' notice about nonrenewal. Most companies will balk at this, since they're rightly afraid you'll stop working hard and will start job hunting as soon as you know you won't be renewed. Instead you can ask for renewal negotiations to begin a certain number of months before termination of the agreement. If they still balk, determine what a cash settlement of equal value would be, and add that to your agreed severance package. For example, if you ask for six months' notice of nonrenewal, or renewal negotiations to begin six months before expiration, and they refuse, ask instead for the company to give you a severance payment equal to six months' salary if the contract is not renewed or extended.

Speaking of severance, the contract should specifically state what you will receive and, more important, the grounds for termination, since severance is generally denied if there is a "for cause" termination. There are hundreds of variations of "for cause," but in general you want to make them as narrow and restrictive as possible. For instance, being arrested should never be a reason for a "for cause" termination. Instead, you should only be terminated in the event of a conviction for certain crimes such as those involving theft or dishonesty or felonies. You also want to get advance notice of other "for cause" violations, such as failing

---

*One client of mine had an employment contract that included a short term loan as part of his agreed compensation. It was understood by all the parties that the loan wouldn't really have to be repaid—it was just an accounting maneuver. However, just as the loan was "due" a new CEO came on board. Rather than formally forgiving the loan, the new honcho decided to use the loan as leverage against my client.

to follow directions or not substantially performing your job duties. The employer should provide written notice and a stated period to cure the problem.

Finally, you want the contract to oblige the employer to pay you in full until the end of the contract term in the event you're terminated without cause. They may refuse, and ask to pay you only until you get another job, or to have their payment reduced by the amount of a new salary. I suggest my clients compromise in this area by agreeing to lowered payments, but only after they've had a certain length of time at full pay to look for another job—say, six months.

I usually stay in the background of these negotiations and have my clients represent themselves. I often only come out of the shadows when there's a physical document that needs to be reviewed. The only exception to this is when the other party is represented by a corporate counsel or business manager rather than a manager or human resources person. If they use their hired gun, so should you.

Equipment

36

One area where a Yourself.com entrepreneur shouldn't cut corners is with equipment.

Since you're relying on your equipment to replace employees and multiply your own efforts you need the most efficient machine possible. You're also trying to get by with using as little space as possible—perhaps even working out of your briefcase—so small size is also important. Finally, because your goals are to make money and to focus on change rather than growth, you don't want to spend a lot of money on fixed assets. How do you answer all these needs? Lease state-of-the-art equipment.

Sure, leasing can be more expensive than buying. But that's only true if you were going to be keeping that piece of equipment for a long time. You're not. You may not need that particular equipment in your next business. And even if you do, to maximize your efficiency you'll need to upgrade it quickly.

Look for short-term—twelve to eighteen months—rather than long-term—twenty-four to thirty-six months—leases. Information technology moves far too quickly to assume the state of the art will stay the same for three years. If you can't get such a short lease, insist on some kind of upgrade option that allows you to turn in your machine for a newer model after eighteen months.

If you're not sure leasing state-of-the-art equipment is worthwhile, rent time and use of state-of-the-art products at Kinko's, Staples, and similar businesses, rather than buying mediocre equipment. For example, it's far smarter for a Yourself.com entrepreneur to pay a premium to use a state-of-the-art scanner and color copier at Kinko's to prepare her media kit than to buy cheaper equipment and do the job herself. That big consulting firm downtown might be able to get by with a less than magnificent package. You can't.

Financial Ratios

37

Wait! Don't jump ahead to the next chapter. Financial ratios don't sound like the most exciting topic . . . and they're not. But a knowledge of them is important for every entrepreneur, and an understanding of a few of them is vital for every Yourself.com entrepreneur.

Financial ratios are relationships between two or more numbers.* By seeing how some specific numbers relate to each other you can get a glimpse into the health of your finances. Yourself.com entrepreneurs, because of their focus on change rather than growth and making money, should be most concerned with two particular financial areas: their short-term cash flow and their profitability. That makes certain financial ratios particularly telling.

First is the quick ratio. This is the relationship between what are called your quick assets—those that can be instantly turned into cash—and your current liabilities. By not including noncash assets such as accounts receivable, inventory, and prepayments you're getting a snapshot of your business's liquidity at this particular moment. Do

---

*You can get the numbers mentioned in this chapter in a couple of ways. You can just ask your accountant for them. However, I think it's more convenient to have your accountant set up your bookkeeping software in such a way that you can call up these numbers and ratios with a few simple commands. I suggest my clients generate a preliminary report containing all these ratios at the end of the second month in each quarter. This gives you a month to take some action if you see there's a problem. Then at the end of every quarter a final report is generated. In addition, I think monthly and annual reports are a good idea as well.

you have the cash to meet your current bills? If you have a quick ratio of at least 1:1 you do. Checking your quick ratio is the equivalent of making sure you have enough money in your personal checking account to pay your monthly bills.

If your business doesn't have enough cash on hand to pay its bills— you have a quick ratio of less than 1:1—it's really not the end of the world. If pressed you can always delay payment and/or convert more assets into cash. However, it is often the first sign there's a serious problem. Either you don't have sufficient working capital, your bills are too high, you're paying your bills too quickly, or you're not collecting your receivables quickly enough. For a Yourself.com entrepreneur these could be signals to make changes or to start looking to change to another business.

Another especially important ratio for Yourself.com entrepreneurs is the collection period ratio. This shows how efficiently your money is being used between its being tied up by extending credit to customers or clients and its being leveraged by getting credit from suppliers.

Divide your net sales by your accounts receivable. Then take the number of days in the year (for simplicity's sake most financial analysts use 360 rather than 365) and divide that number by the earlier result. Finally, subtract from that number the terms you're getting from your suppliers. For example, if you have net sales of $200,000 and accounts receivable of $20,000 the first result is 10. Divide 360 days by 10 and you get 36. That means, on average, your customers or clients are paying their bills within 36 days. If you're getting terms of 30 days from your suppliers subtract that from 36 and you come up with a result of 6.

For a Yourself.com business that is running very close to the edge, a result of 10 or less is good. Anything higher is a sign you're not collecting your money quickly enough, you're paying your bills too quickly, or both. Once again, there are ways to compensate for a poor result, but take it as an early sign of impending trouble.

Your stock to sales ratio indicates how many times your inventory turns over during the year. To figure this out, simply compare your annual net sales by your average monthly inventory. For instance, if you have annual net sales of $100,000 and an average monthly inventory of $10,000 you have a stock to sales ratio of 10:1. That means your inventory turns over ten times during the year. For a Yourself.com entrepreneur who wants to have as little inventory as possible, the higher this number the better. Personally, I like to see my retail clients running so lean that they turn their inventory over at least twelve times a year.

To see whether your pricing works, calculate your profit margin. You arrive at this number by dividing your net income by your net sales. If you had net sales of $200,000 and a net income of $100,000 your profit margin is .50 or 50 percent. Compare this to industry averages you can get from your accountant, but keep in mind that as a Yourself.com entrepreneur your profit margin can be lower than traditional businesses and still be fine since a higher share of that profit is going into your pocket.

Another important ratio is operating expense as a percentage of net sales. This ratio is a great way to keep tabs on your overhead. Personally, I use this ratio monthly and further refine it by looking at individual expense categories as percentages of revenue. This allows me to carefully watch all my costs (see Chapter 17).

Finally, it's important to look at your return on your investment in the business. There are lots of different formulas used, depending on how you define investment. For the purposes of a Yourself.com business I think the best method is simply dividing owner's equity by net (after-tax) profit, and then multiplying the result by 100 to turn it into a percentage. For instance, if you have a net profit of $50,000 and owner's equity of $500,000, you have a return on investment of 10 percent.

What's a good return on investment for a Yourself.com business? It varies. I tell my clients that rather than comparing their numbers to industry averages, they need to compare their return from investing in their business to the return they'd receive by putting the same money into another investment. After all, as a Yourself.com entrepreneur, you are primarily concerned with making money, not simply being in any particular business. If you're an outstanding stock picker and have averaged an after-tax return on your stock investing of 7 to 10 percent, then a 5 percent after-tax return on your business investment* isn't that good. You'd do better simply investing the money. If, on the other hand, you're an average investor who has earned between 3 and 6 percent after

---

*Not counting your salary. After all, if you were working for someone else you'd still be earning a salary.

tax on your investments, then your 5 percent return from your business is outstanding.

If you've been running a tight Yourself.com ship and end up with a disappointing return on investment I'd suggest the best response is to start looking for a new business or to become a mercenary employee. To live rich you really need to get the most bang for your buck. And if that's not coming from your current business you need to get out of it and into another one.

Flextime and Telecommuting   **38**

Flextime and telecommuting are dreams come true for a mercenary employee—and nightmares for a Yourself.com entrepreneur.

Being able to work hours that fit into your personal schedule, rather than the other way around, can certainly help you live rich. So too can working from home rather than your employer's place of business. The added bonus for a mercenary employee is that you also have greater freedom to seek out, and perhaps even take on, other opportunities. But before you set your heart on one of these options, you need to realize just how tough a sale it's going to be.

If you're working for a large, traditional organization, you're bucking years of patterns and practices. Since the dawn of the industrial age managers have been taught to think of employees as lacking all self-discipline and requiring constant observation. By asking for flextime or to work at home you're, in effect, asking the company to give up some control over you.

The best way to accomplish such a tough task is to approach it as a rehire rather than just a minor change. That means you need to sell yourself and your contribution as if you were just walking in the door for the first time. Make sure you have a good reason for your request—such as taking care of your newborn—and then constantly stress your ongoing commitment and dedication to the company. Otherwise your employer will suspect you're looking to goof off, moonlight, or look for another job. Finally, go into this discussion willing to make whatever concession or sacrifice is needed to get your employer's agreement. If you need to buy your own equipment, do it. If you're asked to take a salary reduction, agree as long as it lasts only until you show there will be no decrease in your productivity. If necessary, ask for a trial period. The secret is to have an answer for every possible objection by your employer. But even that won't work if your employer is a Yourself.com entrepreneur.

I tell my entrepreneur clients to reject all employee requests for flex-time and telecommuting arrangements out of hand. Don't even get into a discussion or negotiation. Just say that, based on the nature of your business, such arrangements are impossible. Employees who are adamant will have to find work at a non–Yourself.com company. It's not that I'm worried about employees moonlighting or looking for other work—I'd be disappointed if they weren't. It's that those alternative work arrangements decrease a Yourself.com entrepreneur's chance to live rich.

Your business is potentially so variable that there's no way any employee can know what hours he will need to be on the job and what hours he could take off. You will be on call twenty-four hours a day for your clients. You can't expect the same of your employees, but you need to know that they'll at least be available during all traditional business hours. If they're not, you'll be the one who'll have to pick up the slack, and you'll be the one whose wallet suffers if you can't.

If your employees are working at home you'll be forced to contend with their personal schedules. You're already bending over backward to remain flexible for your clients or customers. You can't do that for your employees at the same time. There's no question of having to choose between your clients' or customers' comfort and your employees' comfort. You can run your business—maybe even more profitably—without employees. Without clients or customers you don't have a business.

Furniture

I'm always amazed at the amount of money people spend on office furniture. Entrepreneurs who have struggled to come up with seed money will go out and spend $1,000 on a lovely wooden desk for themselves. I suppose it's similar to the phenomenon of fledgling businesspeople who fill up their supply cabinets or storerooms: Having supplies and inventory makes them feel like they're really in business.

On the other hand, Yourself.com entrepreneurs know that to really be in business they must minimize their expenses (to maximize their profits) whenever possible. When it comes to furniture, that means spending only where it's important.

If you will be seeing people at your office you'll need to spend a little bit on comfort and image. To minimize these costs consider establishing separate staff and client areas. Clients can be shown into a reception area—functional rather than stylish—and then led to a consulting room with a large table and comfortable chairs. I've discovered that clients feel simultaneously more relaxed and empowered in this kind of conference room setting than they do sitting on the other side of some massive executive desk. This conference room can be shared by everyone who works in the office.

Meanwhile, individual workspaces should be kept spare and utilitarian. Remember: This is a workplace, not a home. Today a desk can be nothing more than a work surface on legs . . . as long as it's the right height for a keyboard. The lion's share of your furniture budget for these spaces should be spent on chairs and lights—only those furniture dollars will translate into greater productivity.

Garb and Hygiene

40

I know you probably don't need a chapter telling you to take a shower and wear clean clothes to work. But as someone who plans on living rich, you *do* need to think more about your garb and hygiene than the average person. That's because you won't have a company or business to fall back on for your identity.

The average employee can rest secure in the notion that there's an image infrastructure behind him. When he visits a customer it's as the representative of, say, IBM. When customers looks at an IBMer, unconsciously they're also seeing and perceiving the image of IBM itself. To a slightly lesser extent, the same is true of the average entrepreneur. While he's more closely identified with his business, there's still an underlying image that can serve as protection. The Live Rich person, on the other hand, is working without a net.

The mercenary employee and the Yourself.com entrepreneur are, for better or worse, representatives of themselves, not some other entity or organization. Therefore your guiding principle should be that nothing should get between the customer, client, or contact and what you say or do; certainly not how you look or how you smell. Anything that distracts attention from what you're doing or saying hurts you. Your goal is for your work garb and hygiene to be unmemorable. The only thing you want to register in the other party's mind is what you said or did.

Your garb should be plain vanilla: clean, classic, formal business wear. For a man that means jacket *and* tie. For a woman it means a suit or a nice blouse with slacks or a skirt. Sticking to the classics will also keep you from becoming a constant prisoner to fashion and will help you save some money. Have your shoes shined frequently. Steer clear of ostentatious jewelry or watches—they may send the wrong message. Don't dress down unless you're going to be alone and working from home all day: You never know whom you could run into and where your next job or client will come from.*

Your hygiene should also be invisible. Don't use cologne or perfume that could bother sensitive noses. Use odorless mouthwash and deodorant. Makeup and manicures shouldn't be noticeable. Add an after-lunch grooming session to your schedule so you can brush your teeth, shave if necessary, and touch up your makeup and hair.

I'm against frivolous cosmetic surgery, but if you have a feature that's truly distracting attention from what you're doing or saying, plastic surgery might be a good idea. Think Barbra Streisand, not Michael Jackson.

---

*I just don't get the concept of dress-down days. If garb doesn't matter at a particular place of business it should never matter, and every day should be dress-down day. But if garb does matter, then every day should be dress-up day. How do the needs of a business suddenly change on Fridays in the summer? Does the company stop doing business on that day? Does it stop dealing with clients? Besides, what kind of mood is created by dressing down? Certainly not a businesslike one. If a company wants to give its employees time to relax during the summer it shouldn't give barbecues or picnics or offer dress-down days. It should give them more vacation time or just let them go home to their family and friends earlier. Remember: Work is work and home is home. Anything that blurs the line is, in my mind, a mistake.

Gifts

41

Either we've all gotten stingier over the years or the nature of business has changed dramatically. Personally I think it's the latter.

Back in the old days when I first went into business it was accepted that the boss would give Christmas presents or bonuses, or both, to all the employees. Managers would give presents to all their subordinates. Vendors would give gifts to all their customers. Everyone in business had huge gift lists and spent a small fortune on bottles of Scotch, baskets of fruit, scarves, and paperweights.

As business has become less paternalistic and more competitive, gifts have become rarer and rarer. Employees still seem to expect something special around Christmas, regardless of how well the company is doing. However, most today are realistic enough to admit they'd rather have a bonus check than a clock radio or an office party. Managers today have fewer subordinates and a less avuncular relationship with those they do have. And fear of having their generosity misconstrued has led many to forgo any gifts to members of the opposite sex. It's more likely they'll just take the whole staff out to lunch one day in December. Vendors, on the other hand, still seem to send gifts to customers, either as thanks for the business or as subtle blackmail for future considerations.

I think that, as part of the Live Rich program, you should swear off all business gifts. In an effort to encourage an employee to adopt the Live Rich philosophy, give her a cash bonus for all her exceptional efforts, stellar performance, or increased productivity throughout the year. Make it clear this year-end bonus is tied to her behavior and the company's financial health, not your generosity or the season. Offer personal good wishes to immediate staff rather than meaningless little baubles. A plate of home-baked cookies with a personal note is far more in keeping with the season than a scarf or tie pin.

Finally, rather than giving gifts to clients and customers as thanks for their business, make a charitable donation instead. For the past five years my office has taken the funds we used to spend on a holiday party and gifts and has given it to a New York City charity for homeless children. We tell our clients about this in our end-of-year letter to them. If you can find a charity that is in some way relevant to your business that's wonderful. If not, just pick a cause that no one could possibly take issue with. Such a gesture is far more meaningful than sending yet another basket from Harry & David. It will set you apart from the crowd. It will burnish your image. And it will be good for your soul.

Headhunters

42

The only time headhunters want to talk to you is when you don't need them.

That's because most headhunters aren't primarily concerned with finding work for you. Their main responsibility is to please their clients. And the easiest way to do that is to steal people away from competitors. Some headhunters bring unemployed people in for interviews simply to fatten up the number of candidates to show their clients they're doing a good job. And despite what that they may tell an unemployed individual, most won't be talking him up to the client. In fact, they may even be using him as someone to sell against.

Headhunters aren't your friends or allies. They certainly shouldn't be confidants: You have to assume that anything you tell them will get back to others in the industry. Some may even be advocates for the company during salary negotiations, perhaps earning a higher fee by bringing you onboard for less money.

All this being said, headhunters do have their uses. They are useful tools for keeping your name in play while you're still employed. They're also wonderful rationalizations for asking for raises, transfers, or employment contracts. Telling your current employer that a headhunter has contacted you about another position is an excellent way to make it obvious that you're valued by others and you aren't deaf to outside opportunities. Six out of ten mercenary employee clients of mine who are contacted by headhunters successfully parlay the approach into more money or a contract from their current employer. Two out of ten get both. And the remaining two also end up with more money . . . by taking the other job.

Hobbies   **43**

Take it from a former workaholic: Hobbies are important. They can provide a way to relax and relieve tension. They make you a more well-rounded person. And they can also help your work.

Hobbies can provide you with a broader perspective on your work life. They can help you place events and situations at work or business into a larger context, allowing you to draw upon solutions and patterns that were successful in other areas. For instance, comparing an obnoxious client's or customer's behavior to that of General Patton not only will help you understand it, but, if you apply tactics similar to those his superior, General Eisenhower, used, you might better be able to deal with him.

Your hobbies can also allow you to pass along information potential employers would like to know, but aren't allowed to ask. A job interviewer would love to know about your health, but can't ask. Letting it be known that your hobby is running marathons will make it clear you're in good health and aren't a smoker.

Hobbies can be used to reinforce your list of skills. Chess and bridge, for instance, require rapid analysis, decision making, and strategic planning. In addition, hobbies, rightly or wrongly, are seen as signs of lifestyle and personality. An interviewer will make one set of assumptions about an avid bird watcher and another about an amateur ice hockey player. Participating in solo sports—like tennis—shows that you're independent, while playing a team sport—such as softball— demonstrates you know how to work with others to achieve a goal.

Finally, hobbies, whatever they imply or the stereotypes they conjure up, provide an opportunity to connect with other people. Most interviewers may not care you're obsessed with the fiction of Patrick O'Brian. But it's always possible the person on the other side of the desk shares your hobby, or has a passing interest in it. Such a connection could give you just the edge you need to accomplish your goal.

Many years ago, when I was president of a Small Business Investment Company, I had to negotiate a major deal with the chairman of a large midwestern corporation. As is my practice, I found out everything I could about the gentleman before our meeting. I spoke with people who knew him and read every article I could find. I learned, among other things, that he was a graduate of West Point and a gourmet chef. At a break after our first round of negotiations, I asked if anyone knew of a good gourmet shop in the area. My opposite number immediately chimed in with some suggestions. We started discussing gourmet cooking; he was drawing on his experience, while I was drawing on . . . my wife Corky's experience. Okay, so I'm not a gourmet cook. But I am married to one. Now that I'm older and wiser, I wouldn't use such a devious technique. Really.

Independent Contractors   **44**

Independent contracting is the future of business.

From an entrepreneur's perspective, hiring independent contractors to do work is far better than having employees. When you hire an employee you not only have to pay her salary but also have to pay her Social Security, workers' compensation, insurance benefits, vacation and sick days, and perhaps contribute to her pension. All those expenses could mean as much as 25 percent of her salary is further added to your labor costs.

Even if an independent contractor charges 25 percent more than you'd pay an employee to do the same work, he's still a better choice. That's because, as independent businesspeople—perhaps even fellow Yourself.coms—they have more of a sense of urgency. Generally, independent contractors do better work, more quickly. They don't engage in office politics and gossip by the coffee machine. They don't bring their personal life to the office with them. They're all business because they're in business for themselves. They come in, do their work as quickly as possible, and move on to the next project.

Be forewarned: You won't get these added benefits simply by calling an employee an independent contractor. Sure, you may get some short-term tax relief, but in the long run, the IRS will make you pay for any questionable maneuvers. There's a long series of tests the IRS applies to determine whether persons are employees or independent contractors, relating to how much control you have over their working patterns and conditions (where do they do their work and when), and how clearly they are in business for themselves (do they have other clients?). Take it from me: The only way you can pass these tests is if the person actually is an independent businessperson.

Rather than trying to convert employees into independent contractor status as a tax dodge, take advantage of it legitimately and go out and hire other Yourself.com entrepreneurs. The IRS will leave you alone, you'll gain added flexibility, and you'll boost your bottom line.

On the other hand, if you're a mercenary employee whose employer asks you to become an independent contractor, use it as leverage to get help in starting your own Yourself.com business or in landing another job. Familiarize yourself with the list of questions your employer would have to answer about your status, and use them to improve your situation. Ask for flextime. Arrange to telecommute. Get assistance in buying your own equipment, including a laptop and cellular telephone. Solicit other clients or other job offers. And most important, ask for a pay raise. Remember, your employer could be saving up to 25 percent of your salary by shifting your status. Make sure you get enough of that money to at least pay for your own benefits. Then go out and get another job or more clients.

Informational Interviews 45

Informational interviews aren't just for job fishing.

As a mercenary employee you're always going to be looking for new opportunities and projects in more than just your own industry or profession. To do that you'll need to have a wide and varied network. One of the best ways to develop an eclectic network of contacts is to solicit and go on as many informational interviews as you can.

Your immediate goal in these interviews is to make a personal connection, not to land a job. That may eventually come from the connection, but don't go into the meeting looking for it to happen right away. Odds are you'll be disappointed—if there was a job opening you'd probably have heard about it. In addition, if you signal that you're really just looking for a job you'll blow your chance to make a good, long-lasting connection.

The best way to get informational interviews is to have a third party intervene on your behalf. When a friend or business contact calls and asks me to meet with someone I always say yes. Why? Because I know he'll return the favor one day. Be creative about finding third-party connections, and don't hesitate to use personal as well as business connections. No man is an island. And in fact, most men have lots of bridges leading to them, including family, business, clubs, profession, hobbies, charities, and church. Any one of those connections is as good as another for the purposes of an informational interview.

If you can't finagle a third-party introduction, make a direct approach. Do all that you can to both flatter the person—"Everyone has told me you're the single best person to speak to about the widget business"—and reassure him—"I know how busy you are, so I'd be ecstatic with just fifteen minutes at whatever time of the day or week is convenient."

The more you prepare for an informational interview, the better your chance to make a lasting connection. Don't wing it: It's a sign of disrespect. If you seem unprepared the other party will cut the meeting short and toss your promotional package (see Chapter 76) into the circular file. Have a comprehensive list of specific questions about the business, industry, or profession you're investigating.

Dress as if you were on a job interview but act more humble. At a job interview you know the other party has a need that you can meet. In this meeting the other party has no need—you do. He is seeing you out of the goodness of his heart. That calls for heavy doses of respect and gratitude on your part.

Begin by asking about his personal history and how he entered the industry. Most people like to speak about themselves but are rarely given the chance to do so without appearing pompous. Listen carefully during the meeting (see Chapter 52). If you can discern some kind of nonbusiness need the other party has that you might be able to meet, make a note of it. Perhaps you hear his son is a football fan and you have season tickets.

As soon as you pick up signals that the other party wants to end the meeting, take the hint. If you don't pick up such signals, but see that your allotted time has run out, start to close the meeting yourself. That will actually improve your chances of staying longer since, out of reciprocal politeness, the other party may offer you more time. Before you leave, ask if he has any recommendations of others you should speak with. If he does, ask if you can use his name when calling.

As soon as possible after the meeting send a follow-up letter offering your thanks. Briefly touch on a couple of the main points of discussion to refresh his memory. Finally, if you can, offer to meet any nonbusiness needs you uncovered. For instance, offer him two of your football tickets. That will guarantee continued conversation. If you didn't find any personal need you could meet, simply follow up within six months asking for another meeting to discuss either your progress or all that you've learned in the interim.

Insurance

46

Are you in the insurance business? If you are, then by all means you should become an expert in business insurance needs—small businesses are springing up everywhere, and they could soon become the industry's fastest growing market. But if you're not, don't waste your time. You're a Yourself.com entrepreneur. Every moment you spend doing something other than making money is a moment wasted. Instead of becoming an insurance expert, hire one.

Ask your professionals and members of your trade association for the names of good business insurance brokers. Not agents, mind you, brokers. There's a difference. An agent is a salesman for one insurer or a couple of noncompeting insurers. A broker is an independent business person who can help you buy from any insurer. He's also more apt to provide you with added services, such as help in settling claims. When you have three names, give them each a call.

Schedule meetings at their offices. (That's another difference between a broker and an agent: An agent will want to come to your home to apply high-pressure sales techniques.) Be prepared to describe your company in a great deal of detail so the broker will be able to determine exactly what types of policies you need and how much of each you need. Depending on your business you may need one or all of the following coverages: business interruption, fire/flood/theft/liability for premises and inventory, professional liability, or errors and omissions. If you need benefits coverage for yourself or employees you might also need disability, health, life, and/or long-term care.*

Don't let a home location deter you from investigating your business insurance needs. Almost no homeowners policy will sufficiently cover damage or loss of business equipment or files. And if you're having customers or clients come to your home you may need to increase your homeowners liability coverage. At the very least you'll need to inform your insurers of the existence of a business to make sure future claims aren't compromised.

Ask each broker to put together a proposal, outlining exactly what insurance he thinks you need, which policies he'd suggest, how the insurers are rated, how much coverage each policy provides, and what each will cost. Once you have three proposals compare them. If there's any one item on a proposal that seems out of line—either much more or less coverage or a far higher or lower premium for the same coverage—ask the broker about it: He has either spotted something the others missed, tried to boost his commission at your expense, or made a mistake.

However, odds are all three proposals will be very close. All other things being equal, choose the least expensive package. Don't worry about making a long-term mistake. You'll be coming back to your broker, and perhaps the other two you didn't hire, in another year to review your coverage needs and costs.

---

*It may make sense to use one or two brokers to help you obtain your personal coverages—auto, life, health, homeowners, and disability—and another broker to provide your business-specific coverages.

Internet Service Providers **47**

I believe it's the Internet that will let many traditional entrepreneurs become Yourself.com entrepreneurs and truly work for themselves. One of the best ways to make this shift is either to move a business from real space to cyberspace or to add a Web site to augment an existing location. So for some Yourself.com entrepreneurs choosing an Internet service provider will (when coupled with designing a Web page—see Chapter 96) become just as important as, or even replace, choosing a location.

Even though your business may be located in cyberspace it still needs a home. Actually, it needs a host: a server computer that's accessible to your customers or clients 24 hours a day, 365 days a year. For most businesses it makes sense to have someone else supply and maintain that computer. (It could turn into a full-time job.) The easiest way to go is to have the same company that offers you access to the Internet—your Internet service provider, or ISP—also keep your site on one of its computers.

There are some interesting parallels between doing business in real space and in cyberspace. The more real space you need for your business, the more you'd have to pay in rent. In cyberspace the more memory you need to store your site, the more you'll pay. And just as you'd want your real space landlord to maintain, repair, and service your location, so you want your cyberspace landlord to maintain your site:

update information, add new pages, and delete outdated information.

At the very least, you'll want your ISP to provide you with all the Internet software you need for free; a point-to-point protocol (PPP) account providing direct access to the Internet; access to the World Wide Web; one or more e-mail accounts; the capability to send and receive files of data through the file transfer protocol (FTP); and access to the newsgroups on Usenet.

My computer-savvy contacts advise using an ISP with at least two T-1 lines, each of which is connected to a different "backbone." You also don't want to share a server with more than nine other sites. They say this offers you the most secure, least likely to crash setup. After all, every moment that your site is down could cost you hundreds of potential clients or customers.

The rapid growth of the Internet has spawned thousands of new ISPs, some good and some flying by the seat of their pants, learning as they go, trying to cash in on the trend. As a Yourself.com entrepreneur you can probably relate to this kind of daring. That doesn't mean you have to fund it, however. Look for an ISP that has been in business for at least three years. I know that doesn't sound like a long time, but in the Internet it's a lifetime.

One of the reasons you're locating your business in cyberspace is that you can be open around the clock. That means you need an ISP that offers twenty-four-hour-a-day access and that has someone on hand all the time to fix problems that could arise.

How fast a connection do you need? The fastest modems available at the time of this writing were able to transmit at 56 kbps (kilobytes per second, or 56,000 bits per second). While there are other options available, such as ISDN lines, a dial-up connection with a 56 kbps modem should be perfectly adequate for almost every Yourself.com entrepreneur.

If you use a local or regional ISP, consider getting a second connection through one of the larger national or international online services. It could serve as a backup if your local provider has a problem. Think of it as paying $20 a month to have a backup location in case a tornado wipes out your headquarters.

Inventory

The ultimate Yourself.com retail business has little or no inventory. Customers should shop and buy based on photographs and descriptions in a catalog or on a Web site. When an order comes in, the entrepreneur contacts his supplier or distributor, who then drop-ships the product directly to the customer. If drop shipping isn't offered, the supplier overnights the product to the retailer, who then ships it out to the customer. That's the ultimate in just-in-time inventory.

If customers aren't ready, willing, or able to buy based on photographs or descriptions, the Yourself.com retailer should have only as much inventory as the customer needs to make a decision. Depending on the type of product being sold, that might be one of each model, or one of each size or color. The "floor samples" are used for marketing only. Customers either have products sent to their homes or return to pick them up on a subsequent trip.

If that's not possible, a minimal inventory that's deeper than it is broad (enough of only a select few items) should be your goal. To the extent you demonstrate expertise you imply that you're carrying only those few products that meet your high standards.

Why am I so against inventory? Well, inventory costs money. First, you may have to buy it before you sell it. Even if you can work out a consignment or delayed purchase system, you'll still need to pay for enough space to display and store your inventory. Then you'll have to spend time managing it. Inventory can't just be left to gather dust. It has to be checked, cleaned, secured, and insured. You may even have to hire someone to take care of it.

In today's world, with overnight shipping and catalog and Internet shopping, there's no reason to go into a retail business that requires you to waste money on more than a minimal inventory. The money you save by eliminating inventory can go directly to your bottom line to help you live rich. That, not full shelves or a big warehouse, should be your goal.

Investor Relations 49

Back when I was president of a venture capital fund I thought I was an expert on investor relations. Every morning I'd pick up the *New York Times* and check to see what my fund's shares were being traded at on the American Stock Exchange. If the price had gone down I'd spend the rest of the day calling and reassuring my primary investors. When there were annual meetings I'd rent impressive wood-paneled conference rooms in palatial bank buildings and arrange for magnificently catered meals. And I would spend months working on the annual report so it read and looked just right. Now I know that every hour spent wining and dining my investors was an hour wasted: I should have been concentrating on the business instead.

Sure, be gracious and grateful to your investors—stockholders or otherwise—especially if they have the power to do you harm. Tell them they can come by to see you anytime and ask any questions they'd like. But spend as little time and money on them as you can. Hold your meetings at your home or your place of business. Bring in sandwiches from the deli if people get hungry. What's most important is that they see you're busy concentrating on the business. That holds true for family investors too.

Actually, as a Yourself.com business you'll probably have few if any outside equity investors. That's good. Equity investors will only slow down your efforts to change quickly. Odds are most of your investors will be family members or friends who have loaned your company money and in return expect interest, a share of the profits, or both. Family and friends are the best investors for a Yourself.com business because, unlike most traditional investors, they're investing in you, not the specific business you're running at the moment. They'll have few qualms about sticking with you whenever you shift directions.

In exchange for that kind of loyalty you owe them complete and total candor. Spell out all the risks as well as their potential rewards before they invest. Then keep them informed of the business's health. Give them written reports every quarter or, if need be, every month. Put as much of your dealings in writing as possible. Whatever their protestations, deep down it will make them feel better.

It's only been in the past year that I think I finally discovered the secret to successful job interviews today: your attitude.

Sure, all the traditional advice about your appearance and manners still holds. Show up on time. Wear classic formal business garb with little adornment. Keep the makeup, perfume, cologne, and hair spray to a minimum. Make sure your breath is fresh, your fingernails are clean, and your shoes are shined. There should be nothing about your appearance that could possibly offend anyone (see Chapter 40). Smile, shake hands, and make eye contact. Concentrate on making the best initial impression you can, since studies show most hiring decisions are made, one way or the other, in the first three minutes. Lean forward in your chair when listening or making a point. Lean back and break eye contact when thinking. Don't cross your arms, and try not to touch your face. Do everything you can to exude class, confidence, and poise.

And the timeworn counsel about answering questions remains true. Think of yourself as a hitter facing a skilled pitcher. Some questions will be fastballs thrown to strike you out. These need to be fouled off—parried so they do you no harm. Other questions will be lobs that are easy to hit. These you've got to hit out of the ballpark by using them to sell yourself, your knowledge of the company, and your skills. Obviously you need to have a good explanation for any gap in your skill base or job chronology. My clients have found that continuing education classes and family emergencies are the best answers for any gaps.

Salary negotiations continue to focus on who is the first to put a number on the table. If you're forced to state your price first it can only go down. If the interviewer is the first to reveal his hand it can only go up.

Most savvy candidates already know these techniques. What separates the winners from the also-rans is, I believe, their attitude. I tell my clients that their goal at this interview isn't to get the job, it's to get the offer. While you're sitting there, concentrate on selling yourself and making that other person see you as the answer to all his hopes and dreams. Forget about whether you *want* to work for this person or whether you'd fit in at the company. Such thoughts will break your sales focus and may lead to questions that detract from your appeal. Concentrate on getting the offer and you're sure to seem enthusiastic and motivated.

Believe me, it's very easy, and very dangerous, to unconsciously signal ambivalence. All it takes is a moment's hesitation or a slight shrug of the shoulders. If an interviewer senses you may not really want the job he'll think you're pompous and will "show you" by not offering it to you, even if you are the best candidate. Conversely, if you work on getting the offer and *then* show hesitation, the employer will want you even more. When he makes the offer he's already hired you in his head. If you don't accept immediately and instead ask for time to speak to your spouse or to consider his offer, he'll start selling you on coming to work for him. If you ask him to reconsider his final salary offer, he may do it in exchange for your immediate acceptance.

Lawyers **51**

Take it from me, lawyers learn little, if anything, about business in law school. They pick up whatever practical business knowledge they possess later in the school of hard knocks.

Yourself.com entrepreneurs need lawyers with business proficiency. Because you won't have a staff of experts, you'll be counting on your lawyer to help you not only set up your corporation (see Chapter 28), but also draft solid, practical contracts for you to use with vendors, suppliers, clients, customers, and perhaps employees. Even if these are going to eventually become boilerplates for you, they still need to be crafted to fit your business's and your own unique needs.

Yourself.com entrepreneurs also need lawyers who have good contacts. Since you're apt to be changing businesses often you don't want someone whose only contacts are in, say, real estate. A generalist lawyer with contacts in a variety of fields will be able to keep up with your changes. And because you don't know what specialized legal needs your might face in your changeable future, you also need a lawyer with her own arsenal of legal specialists.

Finally, since you will always be the personification of your business, you don't want a prima donna for a lawyer. You need someone secure enough to remain in the wings while you're on center stage, offering advice and guidance rather than grabbing the spotlight.

To find a lawyer with all those traits—business proficiency, good contacts, secure ego—you'll probably need to turn to an experienced older lawyer. Unfortunately, such lawyers usually charge the highest fees.* However, with all their experience, they should be able to come up with ways to make their services affordable for you. Once again, you can take it from me.

---

*Lawyers can charge anywhere from $125 to $450 per hour.

Listening   **52**

Most people spend far too little time just listening. Communication
advice abounds about what to say, how to say it, what to wear, and
what to do with your body. In fact, I've devoted three or four chapters
to those kinds of topics. However, there's been little said about listening. That's strange because, in my experience, it's the most powerful
communication tool.

Try this experiment. The next time you're having a conversation
with your spouse or a friend, concentrate on listening closely to what
she's saying. Don't think about all those communication techniques
I've written about elsewhere. Simply focus on clearly understanding
what the other person is saying. Then, rather than responding, repeat
back to her, in your own words, what you've understood her to say,
and ask her if you've heard her correctly. If she corrects you, apologize
and once again repeat her point in your own words.

Once you've correctly stated her point or position, you'll find she's
far more open to your response, whatever it is. Why? Because she
knows you've at least "heard" her and she's gotten her point across.

Once the conversation is over, try to remember what your mannerisms and body language were like. I'll bet that without even thinking
about it you made eye contact, leaned forward, smiled when appropriate, and didn't have your arms crossed. Those actions, when made consciously, are read as open-minded, respectful attentiveness because

they're exactly those actions that we make unconsciously when we listen closely.

I always listen in this manner when I'm speaking with clients. And because I speak quickly and often use legal and financial jargon, I encourage my clients to do the same. I always ask them if they've understood what I've said. Because I've previously gone out of my way to repeat my understanding of their statements, they don't take this questions as an insult to their intelligence.

Make it a practice to listen closely to whatever your clients or customers are saying. And then always repeat your understanding of what they've said before responding so you can be sure you've heard them correctly. This simple practice of attentive listening will do more to improve your work (and personal) relationships than all the sophisticated techniques in the world combined. Start listening, really listening, and you'll start living rich.

Location

53

Location is one of the largest expenses for a business. And for a Yourself.com it's one of the greatest wastes of money. Whether you're a retailer or a service provider, paying for a premium location makes economic sense only if you're going to rely on walk-in traffic. Otherwise, a Park Avenue office, Madison Avenue storefront, and their regional equivalents are just gratuitous ego boosters, not worthy of a serious Yourself.com entrepreneur.

The days when addresses had marketing power are past. Even in New York City, arguably the most status-obsessed market in America, consumers no longer make spending decisions based on a professional's or store's address. In fact, there's somewhat of a backlash against these premium locations. Shoppers realize they're paying higher prices not for added quality, but so the professional or retailer can afford the fancy location. I've found that my somewhat out-of-the-way, anonymous location in an Upper East Side Manhattan condo has actually been a marketing plus. My typical client realizes he's paying for what I do, not where I'm working. And my handful of celebrity clients like not having to contend with crowds.

I'm a big advocate of retail businesses that operate in cyberspace or through the mail rather in real space. Worried about where you'll store your inventory? Don't worry—just don't keep any inventory (see Chapter 48). Always dreamed of having a little store? Wake up. Your goal should be to make money and live rich, not to dust the shelves of Ye Olde Curiosity Shoppe. If the retail business you have in mind doesn't fit the cyberspace/catalog model, you could opt for an out-of-the-way "second-floor" location and devote yourself to becoming a "destination" for your customers. Just take as short a lease with as many options to renew as you can get so you keep your options open. However, I'd rather you just shift your retail business idea one that *does* fit the cyberspace/catalog model.

I'm also a big advocate of locating the headquarters functions of service businesses in the home, and conducting as much business as possible in neutral locations—private clubs, restaurants, hotel lobbies—or in clients' locations. You'll spend less money equipping yourself with all the high-tech information technology you need to run your business from your home and briefcase than you will renting, furnishing, and equipping even a mediocre office location. With Kinko's, Mail Box Express, Staples, and the like everywhere, there are few good reasons that you shouldn't just run your business from your home.*

If you can't run your business from your home and briefcase, consider renting a desk from a business that hasn't followed my advice and finds itself carrying a heavy rent burden.

Whatever money you save by finding a cheaper location can be spent on your marketing efforts—they will have a far greater effect on your bottom line than your location.

---

*So how come I'm not working from my home? Well, I was . . . until my co-op board found out. I guess the procession of people—especially camera crews and messengers—taking the elevator to the eleventh floor tipped them off. They gently informed me that the building bylaws forbid the operation of a business from an upstairs apartment. I had tried to meet clients outside the apartment, but, because of the nature of what I do, it just wasn't possible all the time. Even when I was forced to locate the business out of my home, I still opted for an inexpensive setting and converted a one-bedroom, fourth-floor condo apartment in an otherwise entirely residential building into my office.

Logos

I think every Yourself.com business, even professional offices, should have some kind of logo. Mine is a small architect's rendering of my weekend home in Connecticut. I've used the logo on everything from stationery to brochures to baseball caps that I once had made up for a party. I also have more traditional "lawyer's" letterhead that I use in situations—such as sending an ominous letter on behalf of a client—when I don't think a logo would be appropriate.

Logos needn't be pictures of houses, or trees, or anything representational for that matter. They could be abstract graphics or even your name or initials in an attractive typeface. What matters is that it's unique—rather than a canned graphic or common typeface that anyone could use—attractive, and generic enough to apply to any business you may be in. Of course, that means it should also be professionally designed.

Magazine and Journal Articles

While Americans may bash the media, they still esteem those whose work appears in print. In fact, nothing establishes you as an expert better than penning an article in a magazine or journal. It doesn't matter if you're a Yourself.com entrepreneur or a mercenary employee, or if your article appears in a trade journal or a consumer magazine: A byline sets you apart from the crowd and boosts your personal bottom line.

The best results will come from articles relevant to your work appearing in publications read by your potential customers or clients. For an entrepreneur who sells to or services consumers, that means an article or column in a consumer magazine or newspaper. For an entrepreneur whose customers are other businesses, articles in trade magazines are the best choice. And for an employee looking to make a name for himself, pieces in industry and professional journals will do the job.

Consumer magazines and newspapers are tough to break into, but persistence and networking will pay off. Consider teaming up with a professional journalist. You can provide the expertise while he provides the communications skills and publishing contacts.

Most trade magazines and professional journals are surprisingly easy to crack. They generally have small, overworked, underpaid staffs, desperate for submissions from industry members. The secret is to telephone the editor and simply ask her what she needs. Partnering with another professional can make it easier to crack the more technical and esoteric journals.

When you get an assignment, make sure to use it to your maximum advantage. Since people are more likely to speak to you when you're cloaked in the garb of a journalist, contact industry leaders you may have had trouble adding to your network. Certainly interview your current employer and/or clients and customers as well. Explain to all that you were contacted to write an article and, because of your respect for them, you would like to ask them a few questions.

Once the article appears in print, don't rely on the publication to spread the word of your expertise. Ask for as many originals of the article as you can get. Add one copy to your promotional kit (see Chapter 76) and send out other copies to all those you interviewed and to anyone else you'd like to cultivate . . . including all your existing clients.

One client of mine, a public relations person, interviewed a host of her clients in various industries for a magazine article she wrote five years ago on small business marketing. To this day, copies of the article adorn the walls of four of the people she interviewed. And every one of them is still a client.

Manners and Mannerisms

56

Just as garb and hygiene are especially important for mercenary employees and Yourself.com entrepreneurs, so too are manners and mannerisms. Yours must be perfect because all there is, is you.

Make a conscious effort to smile whenever you meet someone. I know it sounds trite, but it really works. (It also cuts years off your age—see Chapter 10.) People consciously and subconsciously read all sorts of meaning into facial expressions. If you smile they'll perceive you as being warm and caring. Have a stern expression on your face when you say hello and they'll think you're cold and standoffish.

When you're listening to someone speak, or when you're speaking to someone, look her in the eye. Doing that will convey sincerity and honesty more than anything you say. If you have a problem making and maintaining eye contact, focus on foreheads instead. When you pause, break eye contact. That implies deep thought.

Never cross your legs or your arms during a meeting: That signals contrariness and stubbornness. Lean or move forward in your chair when you're speaking or listening to show enthusiasm and interest. Lean back when you pause to think.

Obviously, don't yawn, scratch, blow or pick your nose, chew, or lick your lips during a meeting. In fact, don't even touch your face. I make a point of emptying my bladder, washing my face and hands, inhaling and exhaling deeply, blowing my nose, and then wetting my lips prior to every meeting.

I shake hands firmly with everyone, male or female, when I first meet them. When we say good-bye I do the same, sometimes adding a variation. If the meeting has been a cordial one or I feel the need to reinforce that I care, I'll grasp the other party's hand with both of mine (if it's a female), or place my second hand on his elbow (if it's a male).

I try to avoid all patter and small talk and look to launch right into the business at hand. I don't comment on pictures on the wall or family photos. Of course, if the other party initiates that kind of chitchat you'll have to follow suit to be polite. In that case, respond cordially, but don't open up any new lines of discussion. Hopefully the bullshit will soon come to an end.

I'm not a fan of business lunches (see Chapter 19), but if you're forced into one always let the other party order first. That way you can order a meal similar to his in size and cost. If he orders alcohol don't feel the need to reciprocate. Instead, just order a club soda or soft drink so he's not "drinking" alone. Steer clear of sauces that could result in stains. Take small bites, chew with your mouth closed, and frequently dab your mouth with your napkin. If something gets caught in your teeth, excuse yourself and go to the bathroom before using a toothpick. Finally, don't order anything that requires either dexterity or the wearing of a bib.

Marketing Plans

57

A marketing plan is a sine qua non for every Yourself.com entrepreneur *and* every mercenary employee.

In its most simple form, a marketing plan:

Identifies your target—whether potential customers or employers.

Points out where they can be found—geographically or otherwise, such as in certain associations.

Analyzes the advantages and disadvantages of the various ways they can be reached—cost, power of message, quality of contact, etc.

Lays out a program and process for you to go about reaching them via one or more avenues.

It's vital to approach business and self-marketing in this kind of systematic, proactive manner. If you don't you'll be relying on luck, guesswork, and fate to live rich. I think it's also important to put your marketing plan down in writing and to refer to it often, updating it as needed. This needn't be a formal document. A set of handwritten notes on a legal pad is fine. What matters is that you memorialize your plans.

If you expand this simple marketing plan into a more comprehensive document you can actually use it to test new ideas: either new businesses or new career approaches. To create this kind of laboratory on paper you'll need to:

Fully describe your new business or career approach.

Explain how it's different from your competitors'.

Outline the new idea's advantages and disadvantages.

Roughly estimate the costs involved.

Obviously, every new business an entrepreneur enters will need its own marketing plan, and every employee will need to revise his plan in response to new positions and industry trends. For example, I have one client who has a marketing plan for his restaurant business and another for his acting career. He reviews each annually. Interestingly, his restaurant business's marketing plan has changed dramatically over the years, going through at least four major revisions, while his acting career's plan has been extensively revised only once in more than ten years. Still, he and I will be reviewing it yet again after he finishes his next film.

Memberships

58

Personally, I've never been a joiner. I suppose, like Groucho Marx, I'm dubious of any club that would have me as a member. However, as a businessman, I have been involved in a number of organizations.

I make that distinction because I don't think there's any business or career reason to join social or charitable organizations. If you want to be of service, by all means do so (see Chapter 74), just don't do so with the idea of it being marketing for your business or career.

On the other hand, I think it's important for both mercenary employees and Yourself.com entrepreneurs to join industry and trade associations.

Many of my employee clients are too closely identified with their employer. They devote so much time and energy working for their company that all the scant resources remaining go to their personal lives. I tell them they need to get seriously involved in a trade or industry group so they're seen as industry men, not company men. To do this I tell them to steal time not from their personal life, but from their work. It's actually easy to do. Because they're so strongly identified with the company, their employers view time they spend working on, say, a trade association's policy committee as benefiting the company. It may. But it definitely benefits the individual.

I also try to convince my Yourself.com entrepreneur clients to get involved in either industry associations or generic business groups, like the Young Presidents Organization. Involvement in such organizations does three things that are especially important for a Yourself.com entrepreneur.

First, it gives you and your company a greater perceived size. A very small company can become a "major player" in its business by taking an active and visible role in an industry organization. The advantage of that isn't power, it's that an enhanced presence will serve as marketing for you.

Second, being an active member of a trade group will help you stay on top of the issues and trends affecting your business. You'll be among the first to learn about pressing issues, allowing you to be among the first to position yourself to take advantage of them and to change quickly.

And third, as a "player" you'll be in a good position to establish alliances (see Chapter 11) and partnerships (see Chapter 68) with other companies or individuals in your industry.

Mentoring 59

I've had a string of wonderful mentors throughout my life who have been instrumental in my success. First there was David Osler, who was in the roofing and siding supply business. Then there was Sam Fox, a real estate developer. Finally there's Manny Zimmer, my first law partner. My having them hasn't been either coincidental or a matter of luck. I've actively sought out mentors and I urge you to do the same.

What mentors can do best is give you a crash course in the school of hard knocks. Theory and abstract information can be gained from classes and books. Practical information comes only from doing. You can either go out and slowly gain experience yourself, or you can tap into the wisdom of others. Obviously, the latter is better since it lets you avoid some common mistakes and build on another's experiences.

Having a mentor in business is like having a great guidebook for a trip. You're told which tools you need and which you don't have to bother with. You're advised of the best times to go and the best routes to take. You're warned of the traps and dangers so you can avoid them. And you're coached on what to look for along the way.

Mentors are created, rather than found. Look for someone who's where you want to be or who's doing what you want to do. Tell him of your admiration and respect for what he has accomplished. Explain that you'd like to emulate his success. And then ask how he did it. It's really that easy.

Not everyone you approach will turn into a mentor. Some may not like you. Others may not be interested in passing on their wisdom. Most, however, will be flattered enough to at least give you some good advice. And a handful will take a shine to you, see themselves in your "youthful" idealism, and offer to help you live rich.

Names

60

If Romeo asked me, "What's in a name?" I would have told him, "Lots."

As you must be tired of hearing by now, mercenary employees and Yourself.com entrepreneurs have only their own image to rely on. That makes everything that affects that image vitally important. And your name can have an effect on your image.

My general advice is to call yourself or your company by your given name. That is, after all, who you are, and it is who your business will be regardless of what products or services you're selling. For instance, my company is Stephen M. Pollan, P.C. I think using your full name (Stephen rather than Steve) and a middle initial if you have one adds some weight to what could be a very ephemeral business. Certainly don't use nicknames. What company would you be more comfortable hiring: Stevie Pollan, Inc., or Stephen M. Pollan, P.C.? I rest my case.

Unfortunately, there are instances when using your own name may not be a good idea. I wish we lived in a world where there was no prejudice or stereotyping. However, we don't. If you have a name that implies a particular ethnic, racial, national, or religious affiliation, it could result in you or your business being discriminated against because of it. I'm not suggesting you change your name legally or hide your identity. I'm simply saying that if your name could hurt you, it may make sense for you to vary it in business. For instance, if it's just your first name that could give you problems, you could use an initial instead. If it's both your names you could file a d/b/a (doing business as) form with your municipality and come up with an innocuous name.

Let's say that my coauthor, Mark Levine, had reason to believe there are many individuals in the world of publishing who automatically hated people named Mark. He could start doing business as M. Levine instead. Or he could name his company M.L. Services, hoping to steer clear of anti-Markism.

Negotiating

61

There are hundreds of books out there on negotiating (one of them my own).* Some are learned studies of psychological manipulation. Others are collections of anecdotes from famous "deal makers." Experts have tackled the subject from every angle possible, offering strategies and tactics, tricks and schticks. For entertainment value, you can't beat some of these works. They make great beach reading. It's fun to picture yourself using some of these gutsy techniques and bringing the other party to his knees. Unfortunately, that's not the way for you to live rich.

Don't get me wrong. Negotiating is definitely a part of living rich. You're not going to get more unless you ask for it, and you're not going to get your complaints resolved unless you give them voice. But that doesn't mean you need to arm yourself with secret weapons.

After years of being involved in thousands of negotiations ranging from multimillion-dollar compensation packages to $100,000 real estate deals I've learned that it's only the professional negotiators like me who need tricks and schtick. Mercenary employees and Yourself.com entrepreneurs just need to follow some simple rules.

Establish a clear-cut, reasonable goal.

*The Total Negotiator by Stephen M. Pollan and Mark Levine.

Learn all you can about the other person and the issue.

If the other side hires a professional negotiator, so should you.

Negotiate only with people who want to, and can, make a deal.

Be collegial but direct and straightforward.

Don't worry about winning or losing, just aim to achieve your goal.

I know it doesn't make for great beach reading, but that's all you really need to know. Leave the schtick to me and the other hired guns.

Networking

62

If you were proactive enough to pick up this book it's safe to assume you know that the single best way to find new work and one of the best ways to find new business is to network with other people. However, I've found that most of my clients have misconceptions about what networking really involves.

Networking needn't be going to an industry cocktail party or a meeting of a local social organization, schmoozing, and passing around your business card. There's nothing necessarily wrong with that approach, but networking doesn't have to be so formal.

All of us prefer to do business with people we're friendly with, or with whom we have some connection. When a housepainter lives across the street from you, isn't he the first person you call when you need a new coat of latex on the clapboards? When you're looking for a babysitter for your preschooler, don't you ask your friends' teenage children if one of them would like the job? Well, the same can be true on a grander scale, if you work at it.

Unless you're dealing in narcotics or are a hit man, there's no reason that you shouldn't tell your friends, tennis partners, fellow congregants, and neighbors what you do for a living. Because you're looking to change rather than grow, it's actually just as likely you'll need connections in an area outside your normal business sphere as within. That means these social networks can be just as effective as traditional business networks.

Don't hesitate to talk to people about what you're doing now and what you'd like to be doing. Spread the word. The more irons you have in the fire the better. And keep tossing them in there. You never know when an unexpected pink slip may land on your desk or, conversely, when a good opportunity will come along. Never assume your job or business is permanent, or that the next job or client will automatically appear. Talk to everyone, all the time, about your work. Every time you speak to a person about your work and make a connection, you're in effect adding the contents of their Rolodex to your own. The broader your networking base, and the more active it is, the better your chances to live rich.

Newsletters

63

My quarterly newsletter is intentionally unpolished.

It's a very simple letter sent out to all my past and present clients. In a few short paragraphs I inform them of any recent legal or financial developments that could be important to them—such as changes in the tax law or some recent trends in the job and real estate markets. Then I fill them in on any personnel changes or personal developments in the office—say, a new receptionist or another grandchild on the way. Finally I remind them that I'm there if they need me. That's it. No glossy photos or heavy card stock. My newsletter is just a letter filled with specific news that relates to my clients' relationship to my business.

On the other hand, I have a client who's in the wholesale appliance business who sends out a highly polished glossy newsletter on heavy stock with lots of color photos. In addition to information on developments in her own business, she includes columns on trends in the industry and listings of new products.

What's important about newsletters is that they shouldn't be selling pieces. They should be reselling or reinforcement pieces. Your newsletter is going out to clients or customers who are already on board. It's your promotional package that's going out to potential or new customers or clients. The goal of your newsletter is to keep your customers or clients feeling like part of your "family" and to subtly encourage them to come back soon. Selling material works when you're first trying to attract someone. Once they've hired you or purchased from you they don't want to think you're spending lots of time and money on marketing. They're concerned only with service.

I don't think there's anything wrong with sending your newsletter out via e-mail, as long as that's a common form of communication for your clients or customers. It will certainly be cheaper than a mailing and may actually be read by more people. One final note: If you send the newsletter via snail mail use first-class postage. Personally, I throw out everything not sent first class or better. If it wasn't worth at least 32 cents to send, it's not worth even thirty-two seconds to read.

Office Politics

64

Office politics are a waste of time and energy. If you want to live rich you should work as hard as you can, to make as much money as you can, and then get out of the shop and go live your life.

If you're a mercenary employee, remember my admonition from Chapter 6: Don't make your office your home. In fact, I'd suggest when it comes to office politics and socializing you act like a temp. Smile a lot. Be civil to all. Refuse to take sides. Refrain from gossiping. If you have nothing nice to say about someone, say nothing. If pressed for opinions on people remain noncommittal, even if it makes you seem out of touch.* Don't socialize with people from the office just because they're convenient. If you wouldn't socialize with someone if you didn't work together, then don't be socialize with him. Work is work and life is life. Keep the two separate.

If you're a Yourself.com entrepreneur with employees, do all you can to eliminate office politics. I've done that by trying to eliminate as much office socializing as I can. It sounds harsh but it works.

I make sure there's only room for one person to stand by the photo-

---

*This goes for "gripe" sessions with human resources people and group therapy sessions with company psychologists at the annual corporate retreat. They'll say to speak right up, that nothing will be held against you. But they're lying. Their job is to report on company morale. In effect, they're spies. If you bad mouth someone or complain you'll pay for it one way or another. If you must vent, speak only to a priest in a confessional . . . even if you're not Catholic.

copying machine, fax, and coffee maker so they don't become gathering places. I've made sure the office has no hierarchy. There's me and then there's everyone else. They all report to me. That way, the only possible personality conflict is between them and me. And if we can't get along with each other either they leave or I terminate them. I don't have office parties or hold office gatherings.

I tell all my employees that I believe the best offices or businesses are those that are clean, safe, and physically comfortable, in which people are paid well, do their jobs, and then go home. If they're looking for a social life they should have answered a personal ad rather than a help wanted ad.

Organizational Charts

65

Organizational charts are for management consultants who have never run a real business and petty bureaucrats. No Yourself.com entrepreneur should ever need one. If someone asks you to sketch out your organization's structure, do this: Draw one big X in the middle of the page. That's you. Then, around the big X, draw one little X for every one of your employees. Draw solid arrows from each little X to the big X and connect all the little X's with dotted lines. There's your organizational chart. When you've finished it, you can use it as a coaster for a leaky Starbucks coffee cup.

Outsourcing

66

Outsourcing is a no-brainer for the Yourself.com entrepreneur. By farming out noncore business functions to other companies you'll spend less, get better work, get faster results, be able to terminate with alacrity, and won't need to deal with lots of personal foibles.

One client of mine who runs a boutique advertising agency jumped on the outsourcing bandwagon earlier this year. First he hired an outside firm to handle all his payroll functions. Then he hired a small bookkeeping services company to take care of all his accounts receivable and payable. He is spending about $40,000 less on the two outsourcing firms than he was paying in salary and benefits to his full-time bookkeeper. As if that wasn't enough, he's also got a much more efficient operation.

Both outsourcing firms trimmed away lots of excess fat that, over the years, had accumulated around his bookkeeping processes (things like triplicate records, for example). With his payroll and receivables and payables now being very basic, speed and accuracy increased. An added bonus is it will now be much easier for him to put this work out for bids from other outsourcing firms in the future. And he now has two professional, specialized organizations on the job. After just three months he got an interesting call from his contact at the firm handling his payables and receivables. The outsourcing firm noticed that my client was spending far more on his telephone services than other clients of similar size.

They suggested he look into it. A staff bookkeeper wouldn't have been able to make the same observation, which has resulted in further cost savings.

To get these kinds of excellent results from outsourcing you need to make sure you hire a truly professional firm that has experience working with your kind of operation. That will also minimize problems during the early stages of operations. Shop around, double-check references, and insist on frequent periodic reporting both to you and to your accountant. Work with your outside source on its pricing. It does you no good if it loses money working with you: It won't deliver the results you want and you'll soon be looking for another firm.

As personally admirable as it might be, don't serve as the first client for someone who has just been laid off. By all means open your Rolodex to him, but not your wallet.

Pagers

67

They're not just for drug dealers anymore. If you need to be available to your clients or customers twenty-four hours a day, seven days a week, a pager may be for you.

Rather than relying on an answering service (see Chapter 13), you can set up a voice mail system (see Chapter 13) that forwards your calls (see Chapter 21) to a cellular telephone (see Chapter 23) during normal business hours when you're out of the office, or to a pager during off hours if the matter is urgent.

There are a few caveats, however.

Do yourself and everyone around you a favor and make sure your pager can be set to vibrate as an alarm rather than beep. There's a reason theaters now ask people to check their cellular telephones and beepers rather than bringing them inside.

You must make it your business to return pages as quickly as possible. While I'm convinced that more than half of all "urgent" calls could actually wait until the next day, it's essential from at least a marketing perspective to treat them all as matters of life and death. If the client thought the matter important enough to have you paged, you have to show you think he's important enough to interrupt your dinner, movie, or sleep.

That directly leads to the final and most important caveat. When you get a pager you're crossing the work Rubicon—there's no going back. You're indicating you're willing to put everything else in your life on hold for your work. That's a very powerful statement to make, one that's sure to impress potential clients or customers. But it's one that comes at a potentially huge cost.

Remember: Your goal is to live rich, not work rich. Work should be a means to an end, not an end in itself. You are working to make money you can spend on your life. That requires your having a life to spend it on.

Partnerships

68

A business partnership isn't a marriage or friendship, it's a joint venture to make money.

You don't get a partner because you're lonely. If that's the case get a dog or meet a friend for lunch. You don't get a partner because there's too much for you to do. If your workload is heavy, increase your fees, farm some projects out to other Yourself.com entrepreneurs, or hire a temp.

The worst partner is a clone of yourself. If the two of you have the same skills and experience and the same strengths and weaknesses, you'll only be getting into trouble by forming a partnership. The duplication of efforts will lead to conflict, and the whole will be *less* than the sum of its parts. The best partner is someone who complements you.* He has skills you lack and experience you don't possess; your weaknesses are his strengths. Together the whole must be *greater* than the sum of the parts. If all you do is double your revenue by taking on an equal partner you've made a mistake. You need to more than double revenue to compensate for the loss of total control, the drain on cash flow, and the brake on your speed. For a Yourself.com entrepreneur there's an inherent weakness in numbers.

---

*A silent partner who's just an equity investor is equally good—as long as he stays silent. The minute he opens his mouth—which he's apt to do if revenues drop—he becomes more trouble than he's worth.

Make sure you negotiate a formal partnership agreement and you both have legal representation. Absent a formal agreement, your relationship falls under common or state law, which can be problematic depending on the state in which you live. For example, in New York, if one of the partners dies and there's no agreement in place, the business must dissolve and be divided according to ownership shares.

The most important elements in any partnership agreement are:

The salaries and duties of each partner.

Buyback and buyout provisions, including prices, terms, and negative covenants.

What happens in the event of one partner's disability or death.

How disputes should be resolved.

How the value of the company was determined at the time the agreement was drafted.

Negative covenants restricting the activities of retiring partners.

If you're a mercenary employee who's offered a partnership interest in your company, have an attorney examine the terms carefully. Many times employers dangle some form of partnership in front of valuable employees as a way to force them to sign negative covenants restricting their freedom to work for competitors. It's great to be able to participate in your company's profits . . . as long as that won't keep you from jumping ship for a better opportunity.

Payables

69

Every Yourself.com entrepreneur client of mine asks me the same question about payables: How slowly can I pay my bills? The short answer is: As slowly as you can go without causing pain for your vendors, outside sources, or suppliers.

Let's face it: Every business or individual responds better to people who pay their bills on time. I know I do. I'm sure you do as well. As a Yourself.com entrepreneur the performance of others is just as important to you as your cash flow. All your efforts to burnish your image will be erased if you develop a reputation as a later payer. Sure, you can play games with your payables if you want, pushing the envelope and others' patience in an effort to play the float to your advantage. However, it's going to come at a price, one I think is likely to outweigh any benefit. My advice is that if you need to improve your cash flow, concentrate on your receivables instead (see Chapter 80).

If you find yourself running late because of real cash shortages, rather than a slow-paying policy, don't wait for others to call you. Be proactive. Pick up the telephone and tell your vendors and suppliers you're running late. Don't say you're having problems. Instead explain you're waiting for one particular slow-paying customer or you've been hit with an unavoidable but temporary setback, like a tornado. You're not calling to ask for a favor, just to let them know as early as possible so they can respond accordingly. Nine times out of ten you'll get a better deal by forewarning them than if you wait for them to contact you.

Performance Reviews

Performance reviews should be just that: reviews of an individual's job conduct. They should not be salary reviews as well (see Chapter 83).

For a mercenary employee, a performance review is actually a very bad time to ask for a raise. First, it's not your forum, it's your manager's. That means you have no control over the timing and little chance to set the agenda. And second, any efforts you make to push for an increase could actually backfire, leading to a less positive review than otherwise, since your manager will be forced to look for reasons not to give you a raise.

I tell my mercenary employee clients to instead use performance reviews as barometers of their status. Since you should always be looking to change rather than grow, your review can be used to determine how quickly you should jump to another opportunity. A negative review, for instance, is a warning sign that you should get out of there ASAP, certainly before the next review. A positive review that doesn't offer you new opportunities is a signal you've maxed out and need to find another opportunity within the year. A review that's positive and that also offers you chances to change while staying with the company is an indication there are still internal opportunities to exploit. Don't get complacent and stop looking. But don't jump at the first thing to come along either.

In every one of your performance reviews, make sure to express, as early as possible in the conversation, how grateful you are to the company and your manager for giving you the chance to work and learn. I know it sounds corny, but it works.

If you're criticized, don't argue facts and never disagree with opinions unless they're based on hearsay rather than the manager's personal perceptions. Instead of debating, offer reasons or rationalizations, ask for suggestions to help you improve, express your profound thanks, resolve to improve, and then go home and gear up your personal marketing campaign.

For a Yourself.com entrepreneur a performance review is a chance to warn, correct, or encourage an employee as part of your efforts to boost your bottom line. Employees who aren't producing up to expectations are a drain on your wallet. As a Yourself.com entrepreneur you're running a tight ship on a short trip so you need to minimize any damage and deal with problems right away. That's why I suggest you review every employee within three months of hiring and then at regular six-month intervals.

I use that first review to put on notice any employee who isn't producing up to expectations. Provide specific examples of what they've done wrong and how you expect them to improve. Subsequent reviews are to offer fine-tuning suggestions or to alter the individual's work profile based on changes your business is going through.

Schedule performance reviews for "first thing Monday morning." That indicates the importance you place on them, and gives the employee a chance to act on your suggestions right away.

Don't offer praise and then criticize constructively, a pattern you'd use with a child or spouse. This is an employee, not a family member. Yours is a business relationship. Keep it on that level. Don't worry about sugarcoating your message or pulling your punches. Say you want the relationship to work but you have some concerns, and then go right into your points. Remember: This is a performance review, not a therapy session.

I think it's great to memorialize your general policies toward customers, clients, vendors, and suppliers. It can only help you keep on track. However, there's one huge caveat: Do not create a general policy document for your employees unless it is required by law (because of the number of employees).

Just because you've seen a book or software package that has a boilerplate employee handbook is no reason to create one. If you have a policy manual dealing with employees it could become an implied contract between you and anyone you hire. I'd much rather you draft individual employment contracts or termination agreements (see Chapter 93) with specific employees than offhandedly create some kind of blanket agreement. Avoid those general boilerplate agreements and talk to your lawyer instead (see Chapter 51).

Press Releases   **72**

Press releases are the Lotto tickets of public relations. Sure, sometimes they result in a story or item. But most Yourself.com entrepreneurs are wasting their time, energy, and money sending out releases to media outlets.

The first dirty secret of press releases is that most of them end up in the garbage unread. They're generally scanned by editorial assistants fresh out of college, who are told to pass along only "important" releases to the senior editors. The exception are releases intended for columns that simply list upcoming events, new products, industry promotions, or other small items. To get coverage in any other part of a publication invariably requires a personal contact with the writer or reporter, either via a successful cold call or a public relations person.

The second dirty secret of press releases is that there's usually some kind of leverage responsible for those that are used. Perhaps the public relations person has done a favor for the editor in the past. Maybe there's an unspoken quid pro quo: The editor gets a sample of the product, strictly for "review purposes," of course. Or it could be that an ad is purchased with the understanding that editorial coverage will come along as a bonus.

By the way: You didn't hear these dirty secrets from me.

Pricing

The instinctive reaction of almost every Yourself.com entrepreneur is to take advantage of his lower expenses and overhead and price his products and services below those of his competitors. This is one instance when you should definitely go against your instincts.

As a Yourself.com entrepreneur you are fundamentally selling yourself rather than your products or services. Offer them at a low price and you're signaling you aren't the best. That's an invitation to failure. All customers and clients, whether they're consumers or other businesses, crave superb personalized attention as well as top-quality products and services. And they are willing to pay for it.

Look at the success of premium brands like Starbucks and Ralph Lauren. Can you get cheaper cups of coffee and less expensive flannel shirts? Sure, and places that offer those discounted items are doing well too—just look at Costco and Wal-Mart. But as a Yourself.com entrepreneur you're never going to be able to compete with those who offer lower prices. You simply don't have the economies of scale necessary. Instead, play to your strength. You can provide even more personalized attention than a Starbucks or a Ralph Lauren. You can make individual blends of coffee for customers. You can custom-tailor flannel shirts to fit a customer's exact measurements. And you can charge more by doing so.

I don't mean to get bogged down in java and jodhpurs. The principle applies to all products and services. D. Lee Carpenter from the consulting firm Design Forum has written that all customers can be divided into two types: left-brain and right-brain. Left-brain customers are looking for low cost and low service—they like to go to Costco, Wal-Mart, and other discounters—while right-brain customers are looking to satisfy creative and emotional needs. They're the folks who buy their cup of coffee at Starbucks rather than 7-Eleven. They're also the folks you should be looking for.

The very nature of your business lends itself to the kind of highly personalized and customized products and services that attract right-brain customers and clients. And that directly leads to premium prices. Which conveniently enough leads to high profit margins, which is exactly why you became a Yourself.com business in the first place. It's all fits together very nicely. You are a top shelf brand. Price yourself accordingly.

Having set a premium price on your products and services, make sure you're up front about it, and stick with it. Discuss your prices and fees as early as possible in your conversations and presentations. Don't defend it, simply demonstrate why you're worth it. Still, there will always be some clients and customers who quibble with your price. Don't bite. You have no excess overhead to cut, and few if any staff people to pass work on to. If you're selling products, your only options are to suggest they wait until you have a sale, or consider floor models or reconditioned items. The only way you can lower your fee for services is to do less work.

Actually, that's often a good technique. One tax accountant client of mine deals with fee-quibbling clients by asking them to do more of the work themselves. He tells them what software package to use, and offers a prepared list of expense and account categories for them to use. He then asks them to e-mail their files to him by a certain date. By having them do most of the prep work, he can spend less time on their returns than he normally would. It's a wonderful technique. He maintains the credibility of his hourly fee and keeps up his image, while expanding his market to include clients he'd otherwise lose. That's a true live rich solution.

Pro Bono Work and
Charitable Volunteerism

74

I firmly believe in giving to charity. I'm convinced there's some kind of cosmic balance in the world: For you to keep the good things you have, you need to give some of them away. However, I don't believe any of this applies to your business life.

By all means dedicate as much of your personal money, time, and energy as you wish to doing good deeds for others. But every penny and minute of your business resources devoted to such noble efforts should have a real, measurable return. If your pro bono work helps your image and leads to more business, great. If your sponsorship of a charitable event is effective marketing, terrific. Otherwise, volunteer on the weekend or write a check from your personal accounts. To live rich you need to concentrate on making money through your work and business. If for you to live rich you also need to give some away, do it on your own time.*

---

*One note for mercenary employees: Don't think your charitable efforts will help your standing with your employer. He may give you a plaque and pat you on the back for them, but he won't give you any more money or opportunities because of them. And they certainly won't make your position any more secure.

Professional Relations 75

All entrepreneurs depend on their professional team to provide expertise they lack and wise counsel. Yourself.com entrepreneurs, with fewer staffers than traditional entrepreneurs and running on a tighter budget, must lean on their pros even more.

That's why you should always hire the most seasoned professional you can find: someone with years of experience working with entrepreneurs just like you. It's not your place to give a break to your nephew who just graduated law school. You can't afford to have someone learn from mistakes made on your behalf. If you want to help your nephew buy him some law books instead.*

Similarly, don't try to save money on your professionals. Having a tax preparer operating out of a temporary storefront at the mall prepare your returns is going to end up costing you more long-term than you save short-term. If money is truly an issue, discuss it with the professional. Most will come up with ways to lower your bill, perhaps by having their staff, or even you, do more of the work.

Experienced professionals offer an added bonus: their Rolodex. A professional with lots of contacts can serve as an integral part of your marketing program. He can talk you up to his contacts while you do the same for him. I've gotten client referrals from all my professionals, even my dentist and doctor.

*I know this may seem self-serving coming from an experienced, older professional. However, I truly believe it. That doesn't mean I never use young professionals. I actually have a regular group of young professionals I farm work out to. But in most cases it's for very technical matters dealing with new developments and cutting-edge topics in accounting and investing.

Promotional Kits

Résumés aren't sufficient for mercenary employees (see Chapter 81). Brochures and pamphlets aren't enough for Yourself.com entrepreneurs. In today's world of digital multimedia every employee and every entrepreneur now needs to have his own promotional kit as well. This kit should be based on the "media kits" public relations firms send out to herald their clients.

It begins with an eight-and-a-half-by-eleven-inch two-pocket folder. Your name (see Chapter 60) and logo (see Chapter 54) should be on the outside cover. On the inside you should insert a preprinted Rolodex card and/or a business card. Information sheets about you as an individual should be placed on the left side of the folder, while information about what you do or sell should be on the right side.

Inside there should be a single-sheet prose biography of you with a conservative headshot photo scanned onto the page. There should also be a formal curriculum vitae or résumé, this time without a photo. Separate sheets should list your skills and achievements, citing specific projects and numbers whenever possible.

Include a separate list of references. If clients, customers, or former employers have written or offered words of praise, prepare a testimonial sheet. Awards and honors should be highlighted separately as well. Personal information, including your hobbies and interests, should be on another sheet. That may be sufficient for most mercenary employees. Yourself.com entrepreneurs, on the other hand, need to add more.

Whatever business you're in, there should be a page offering a description and history of the business.

If you're in a service business, a list of services along with description of each should be provided. Add appropriate graphics if they're available. Average fees should be noted on a different sheet.

If you're in a product business, each of the products or lines you sell should have its own sheet, which includes full descriptions, photos or drawings, and prices.

If you're a published author, artist, or performer, there should be a separate sheet or sheets listing your publications, shows, and performances. Covers of your books or stills of your work or performances can be scanned in as graphics. Copies of articles by and about you and your work (if positive) should be included. (This goes for mercenary employees too.)

Supplements to this kit could include video or audio tapes of performances and speeches you've given or appearances you've made; CDs or floppy disks with electronic copies of presentations you've made and/or HTML versions of everything included in the kit.*

Not all of this material need be included every time you prepare a promotional kit. In fact, the whole idea is to have a package that's simultaneously comprehensive and easily changeable. Drop or add a product or service from your line, and all you should have to do is change a couple of sheets. Change your business entirely, or go from entrepreneur to employee, or the opposite, and you'll still be able to use almost all your personal pages.

For instance, the package a photographer client of mine gives to consumers contains all the material about his studio business, but just a listing of the books and magazines his work has been in. The copy he sends to media people contains only a couple of sheets about his studio business, but extensive information on his book and magazine credits, including both a glossy collagelike print compilation of his best work and a separate digitized collection of shots on a diskette.

Don't skimp when it comes to preparing this kit. Have it designed professionally, preferably by the same person who did your logo and stationery. Use good-quality paper. If it makes sense, use a second color in

---

*HTML is hypertext markup language, the format used to display information on the World Wide Web. In fact, you might want to prepare this promotional kit and your personal Web site simultaneously.

your printing and full color in your graphics. This is one of the few areas where Yourself.com entrepreneurs and mercenary employees should spend more money than their more traditional peers. It's an investment that will pay off. It will set you apart from everyone else, and if it's responsible for winning you just one good client or landing you one more job it will have more than paid for itself.

For a mercenary employee there's more than one way to change rather than grow. The most obvious is to shift companies. But the traditional maneuvers of getting a promotion or making a lateral move still have merit, as long as they're viewed as changes rather than steps up some kind of hierarchical ladder.

Even though your focus should always remain making money, a new title or a move into a healthier or more promising part of the industry can quickly translate into a salary increase. If nothing else, a different title that moves you into a higher management level should put you in a better position to ask for a higher starting salary from your next employer. The market value of directors of marketing, for example, is higher than the market value of assistant directors of marketing.

The best way to ask for a promotion is to present yourself as being ready to contribute more to the company's bottom line. Stress how much more you'll be able to do for the company in the new position. Never present the promotion as something you deserve for past contributions: That's like asking for a medal. In addition, never couple the promotion request with a salary review. If you ask for a raise as well, you detract from your claims of boosting the bottom line. Besides, you'll usually end up getting one or the other, not both. Wait until you've established yourself in the new position before asking for more money.

For a mercenary employee lateral moves can be just as beneficial as promotions—if they move you into a more promising part of the business or give you the chance to add new skills and achievements to your portfolio. For instance, a lateral move from a computer software company's spreadsheet division to its Internet division could be a superb move.

The secret to successfully making a lateral move is to first create a demand. Before speaking with your superior, contact the department or division you'd like to move to. Make your case directly and turn them into an advocate for the transfer. Not only will this increase your chances of successfully shifting, but it will ensure you'll be accepted and able to hit the ground running when you do make the jump.

To overcome the most common objection to either promotions or lateral moves, have a plan and series of suggestions about who can take your current place. Offer to work overtime to make the transition a smooth one.

Punctuality

78

The best advice is often the simplest. For a mercenary employee the single most effective thing you can do to impress an employer is show up early.

Every entrepreneur and manager knows that the best time to get work done is before the telephone starts ringing and before the crowd arrives at the office. That's why you'll find me at my desk by seven-thirty. That's also why I tell clients who need to get in touch with an executive to call very early in the morning when he's likely to pick up his own telephone.

When you show up early, here's what happens. The owner or manager sees you. The first time he sees you he's simply impressed with your diligence and sense of urgency. You've become the star employee by default because you're the only one there to shine. Once he realizes this is a regular pattern, and since there's no one else around, he soon comes over to say hello. You chat for a few moments. After a while you're saying hello and talking every morning. Who knows, maybe you're sharing a cup of coffee. Even if you don't become java buddies, you've gotten great "face time," a personal connection has been made, and your image has gotten a boost.

Late risers may wonder if the same holds true for staying after hours. Well, I'm afraid it doesn't. Having shown up early in their effort to live rich, most managers and owners want to get home to their families as

soon as they can. That usually means they're out of the door around closing time. If your boss sees you sticking around late he's not going to
think you're hardworking. He'll wonder what you're doing wrong that
you couldn't get your work done during the day. And he'll worry that
you're coming in late, since he certainly didn't see you there at the crack
of dawn.

Reading

79

Obviously you're a reader. That's good. Whether you're a mercenary employee or a Yourself.com entrepreneur, reading will play an important role in your being able to live rich. When you're well read you appear even smarter than you are. That translates into more business and greater success on the job.

You don't need to boast of your reading, or devour every book, magazine, and newspaper available. Your knowledge will come out naturally (as will others' lack of knowledge) during normal conversation. Read one daily newspaper to keep up on current events. Pick up a weekly newsmagazine to get perspective on the news. A weekly or monthly cultural magazine will add color and spice to your thinking. Scanning one industry or professional journal should be sufficient.

I'm obviously a fan of how-to books, but I think you should also read novels, poetry, history, science, biography, or anything else that sparks your imagination. While reading should serve as indirect marketing for you, it should also add dimension to your thinking. Reading about different fields, people, time periods, and places gives you a broader perspective on the world. That can make your more creative and innovative. And creativity and innovation will certainly help you live rich.

I learned everything I needed to know about accounts receivable from my good friend Kenny Tillman.

I've known Kenny since we were both seventeen years old, and for more than 20 years he's owned and operated a consumer electronics store in New York City. We speak on the telephone at least twice a month. Like most of his friends, I also make all my electronics purchases at Kenny's store. What's always impressed me is that, like clockwork, one week after I get a bill from Kenny he calls to ask me to pay up. He has never been afraid to bring up money, even though we're the best of friends. I once asked him about it, and he in turn asked me, "What's one thing have to do with the other?" He's absolutely right.

As a Yourself.com entrepreneur you cannot be timid about asking for payment of past due fees or bills. You need to separate your relationship with the customer or client from the money issue, just like Kenny Tillman. Don't fall into the trap of being afraid that by pressing for payment you'll lose the customer or client. If the slow payer does leave you, you're actually better off; you were being taken advantage of. Obviously the only thing that was important to that client or customer was being able to play the float at your expense. That's not the kind of client or customer you want.

By letting fear of losing business keep you from asking for payment, you're investing power in a person who owes you money. If you fall into that pattern you'll soon find that the more money someone owes you, the more power you're investing in him. Soon you'll actually be treating your worst customers or clients better than everyone else.

If when pressing for payment you're offered a tale of woe, don't accept it as a justifiable reason for slow payment. Instead of being "understanding," offer advice. Explain how you've dealt with similar situations by borrowing money or tapping into your personal funds to keep from paying late. The message will be clear: Pay up.

Résumés

I hate traditional résumés. They're designed to be one-sided, offering the reader just the information he needs to screen candidates out. That's why I tell my mercenary employee clients to prepare promotional kits instead (see Chapter 76).

Of course, part of that kit should be a sheet offering your career chronology. All you need to do is make sure any gaps in it are positives, not negatives. If you spent those two months between jobs in 1983 traveling through Europe, say so. Travel broadens the mind, gives you an opportunity to learn about new cultures, and helps you pick up a second language. Those four months between jobs in 1994 weren't time off, they were part of your program of continuing education, since during that time you took an intensive course in economics at the local community college.

Don't worry about defending a history of "job hopping." Any employer who has had his head out of the sand for the past five years knows that's actually a positive trait. And if someone who's interviewing you doesn't realize that, make him aware of it. There's no reason to be defensive about your history. You've been in constant demand. Companies have continually sought you out. As a result you've been able to move from one opportunity to another. Yours is a track record of successes, not failures. It's the sign of a victorious mercenary employee.

Salary

Here's the Live Rich philosophy on salaries: Pay yourself as much as you can and everyone else as little as you can. Of course, it's not quite that simple in practice.

To attract decent candidates you'll need to pay your employees enough so that you're competitive with other comparable businesses. You can find that out by speaking with other employers, consulting your trade association, or checking with an employment agency. I think it's only right to offer automatic annual or biannual cost-of-living increases so your employees don't lose ground in real terms. On the other hand, I don't think you should increase salaries just for seniority, or give merit raises (see Chapter 83). You're looking to attract and hire decent, not great, people, for one to three years, not a lifetime (see Chapter 33).

When it comes to your salary you need to be a bit more circumspect than the simple philosophy might indicate. Sit down with your accountant and try to determine how you can make your aggregate compensation of salary and benefits as large as possible, while keeping it as sheltered from taxes as possible. Bear in mind that while income tax evasion is a crime, income tax avoidance is not. In fact, some would say it's your patriotic duty.

Salary Reviews

The rationales for successfully asking for salary increases have changed dramatically in just the last five years. For a mercenary employee today there's only one good reason to ask for a salary increase: You're not being paid the market value for the work you do. Use any other rationale, even those that may have worked for you in the past, and odds are you'll come out of the meeting empty-handed.

Seniority is no longer sufficient reason for an increase. And, in fact, it never should have been. Just because you've been doing something for a decade doesn't mean you should get paid more for it than someone who's doing the same work, but has only been at it for a year.

The only regular salary increases you should count on are for jumps in the cost of living. If you haven't gotten an automatic cost-of-living increase in over a year you're fully justified in asking for one, based on the time that has elapsed. However, this isn't a raise—it's keeping you from falling backward—so don't treat it as one. Frame it as a necessary maneuver to keep you in place and you shouldn't have a problem getting it.

Proficiency isn't even a good reason for a raise any longer. You're now *expected* to be good at what you do. If you're not, you'll be terminated. The only skill-based increase that's possible is if you add a new skill to your repertoire, take on added tasks and responsibilities, and thereby move yourself into a new work category, one with a higher market value.

Doing an extraordinary job, and as a result, boosting the company's bottom line, merits a bonus, not a raise. By all means ask for a bonus if you've saved the company money, increased revenues, or saved time. You'll be much more likely to get the bonus than you would be to get a raise based on your efforts. After all, the bonus is a onetime event— the raise would be a permanent increase in the company's labor costs. Boost the company's bottom line again in the next six months, and you can go in and ask for yet another bonus.

The only raise request that works today is that you're not earning market value for your work. Why? Because if you can show an employer that he's not paying market value for the work you're doing, he'll realize that if you left he wouldn't be able to replace you without increasing the position's salary. And if he'd have to do that anyway, he might as well do it for you, since you're presumably already doing the work very well. If he has to bring in someone new he'd lose time and money during the transition period. Finally, he also knows that, since you're obviously a mercenary employee, if he doesn't pay you market value you'll go elsewhere to get it.*

Of course, proving you're not getting what you're worth isn't easy: You'll need to conduct your own compensation survey. Call head-hunters and ask them for estimates. Speak with employment agencies. Telephone your peers and get their feelings. Check with professional and industry associations. Scan employment ads in industry journals, and while you have the magazine out, get the telephone number of the editor. Call him and ask his advice too; he may know of proprietary surveys you could read. See if you can find any data from any federal or state agencies or departments. Analyze your research, draft a concise, cogent argument for your position, and put it down on paper. Make sure to cite your sources. That will not only add substance to your

---

*Another very effective method of getting a raise is demonstrating you're not getting the market value for your labors by telling your employer you've just received another job offer for much more money. Many employers will meet or beat such offers to keep you, particularly if the job offer came from a competitor. While very effective, this maneuver does have some risk. If your current employer balks at meeting the new offer, having made the threat you'll be forced to jump ship. Even if your current employer offers you a raise as a result of your outside offer, he may feel as if you've extorted it from him, and you could be marked as a disloyal troublemaker who'll be the first one let go in the future. Showing the outside offer came unsolicited—perhaps via a headhunter—and having a clear financial need—a new baby, for instance—can help mitigate the damage . . . but don't count on it. That's why you must make sure the increase is sizable—it has to be worth the risk.

argument, but will also subtly show you've got the necessary contacts activated if you must look for another job.

Present your memo at a meeting set up specifically for this purpose. Never couple a salary review with either a request for a promotion (see Chapter 77) or a performance review (see Chapter 70). I always tell my clients to push for early morning meetings on Tuesdays, Wednesdays, or Thursdays. They present the best opportunities for getting your superior's undivided attention.

If you're turned down for any reason other than that the company doesn't have the money right now, it's time to look for a new employer. Do you really want to live rich? Then you can't work for someone who isn't willing to pay you fair market value for what you do. If your employer doesn't think you're worth the going rate, either you or your position will soon be eliminated.

If you're told the money simply isn't there right now, look for an assurance that it will be there soon, and that when it is available you'll get your raise. Set a specific date for another meeting to revisit the issue. If you're offered other forms of compensation, feel free to consider them. Anything that provides you with more time is often an acceptable substitute for money. For example, increased vacation time, a telecommuting arrangement, or some type of flextime schedule all offer more opportunities to actually live rich, as well as time you could use to pursue other ways to make money. Titles and other nonfinancial perquisites may be of some help to you in the future, but they're no replacement for money or time today, so don't accept them as a substitute for a future raise.

When a Yourself.com entrepreneur is approached by one of her employees asking for a salary review it's a sign she's made a mistake. I advise Yourself.com entrepreneur clients to be proactive when dealing with employee salaries.

If you're satisfied with their work, give your employees an automatic cost-of-living increase every six to nine months. Unless they're not working out and you plan on terminating them, they deserve to earn at least what they were paid when you hired them. If you temporarily can't afford the increase, say so and explain you'll revisit the issue as soon as the bottom line improves. If you believe an employee is starting to cost more than he's worth, say so. Suggest he either develop ways to increase the company's profitability or find another position. If he does neither, terminate him and hire someone new at a lower starting salary.

By proactively offering cost-of-living increases you'll boost morale and, I believe, end up paying less in labor costs. Few employees will respond to an unsolicited raise with anything more than a thank-you, particularly if the increase is made as a Friday afternoon surprise. If they do ask for more, simply explain your attitude toward increases of more than the cost of living.

I think raises of more than the cost of living are justified only by increases in the business's bottom line. If an employee takes on more responsibility, freeing you up to generate more business, or generates more business on his own, reward him. I think the best way is to somehow tie his salary increase to the increase in profits. In my own office I've done this by offering year-end bonuses based on increased profitability, on top of the periodic cost-of-living increases. In years when profitability hasn't increased I simply haven't given bonuses. I don't think there's a better way of simultaneously making clear the direct link between salary and profits and motivating employees to boost the bottom line.

Scripting

84

I believe in planning and scripting every single important conversation I have whether it's with a client, an employee, or my wife. There's nothing wrong with preparing for such conversations. In fact, I think that by *not* preparing for important dialogs you decrease your chances to live rich.

I go to great lengths to prepare for my conversations, and I help my clients do the same. I make copious notes about goals, think about tactics, and then draw charts illustrating the course I want the conversation to go. I spent time going over exactly what my client or I am going to say, and how we'll deal will all the other party's possible responses.* Then, I encourage my clients to prepare notes for themselves on three-by-five cards that they could bring with them to meetings.

You needn't go to the same lengths my clients and I do, but I strongly suggest that you do at least five things before every important dialog.

First, do everything you can to take control of the situation. That doesn't mean you monopolize conversation or bully the other person. It just means that, through your choice of words and reactions, you

---

*Because I've had such a positive response to this part of my consulting practice, three years ago I compiled many of my scripts and published them in a book titled *Lifescripts*. I've also edited a series of three subsequent books of similar lifescripts.

frame and steer it in the direction you want it to go. It could be as simple as making the first move, and thereby forcing the other person to respond. Or it could mean responding in such a way that the other person is forced into retorts you're prepared to address.

Second, clearly say what you want. Whether it's because we don't want to be viewed as demanding or we're afraid of being turned down, most of us beat around the bush, imply, and drop hints, rather than coming right out and saying what we want from someone else. If you want to live rich you can't rely on other people to infer. Force people to respond directly.

Third, learn to show your power before you use it. Subtle demonstrations of potential power are often more effective than the immediate use of that power. For instance, if you're a restaurant patron you have two powers: your ability to make a scene and your willingness to pay your bill. By calling over a waiter or maître d' and whispering that you're unhappy with your meal and would like another, you demonstrate that you're aware of your power to make a scene, but are holding it in check until they've had a chance to respond. If you actually raise your voice and make a scene immediately you will have used up all your ammunition. Other subtle displays include saying things like "I'm a longtime customer and would like to continue our relationship," or "The last thing I want to do is hire someone else to finish this project."

Fourth, withhold, absorb, or deflect anger. Displays of anger are self-defeating. They say: "I've no real power, so all I can do is make noise." Hold your temper whenever possible. When you're met with anger, either absorb it by acknowledging it—"I can understand your being angry. I would be too"—or deflect it by suggesting it's an odd reaction and must therefore be based on something other than your request—"I don't understand why you're getting angry at me. Have I done something else to bother you?"

Fifth and finally, try to have the last word. It could be expressing thanks for getting what you wanted, asking for reconsideration of a rejection, pushing for another meeting, or saying you'll call back if you couldn't get a definite answer. Whatever's involved, having the last word makes sure you retain the control over the dialog and can therefore end it on the most advantageous terms. The only exception would be a situation when it's important for you let the other party think he's still in control . . . even though he's not.

Seed Money

85

Banks and other institutional lenders have never been willing to provide start-up funds for small businesses. And they're sure not going to be feeling any friendlier toward Yourself.com entrepreneurs. Sure, they'll lend you money . . . as long as you use your house as collateral or use your personal credit. In other words, they'll deal with you, just not your business.

So where can you turn for seed money for your Yourself.com business? Tap into your savings, including your retirement funds. Max out your credit cards. See if you can get a home equity line of credit. Ask your parents to give you your inheritance early. Borrow from siblings and friends—if they don't have confidence in your future and honesty, who would? Play the lottery. In other words, you have to do what every other American entrepreneur has been doing for the past two centuries: beg, borrow, and . . .

Signage

86

Fancy signs don't tell the world your business is successful.

For most Yourself.com businesses, signage serves only one function: It tells customers they're in the right place. The only businesses for which signage serves any kind of marketing role are those that rely on attracting walk-in trade. And if you're a Yourself.com entrepreneur in that kind of business, I'd still suggest you steer clear of expensive signs. Investing thousands of dollars in signage for a business you may abandon in a year is crazy. Instead, look into equally noticeable but far less expensive options, such as flags and banners. You could get a magnificent, eye-catching banner for your chocolate-covered-bagel stand for a less than a tenth of what a neon sign would cost you. So what if the banner is tattered in two years? By then you'll be selling frozen-yogurt-covered bananas on a stick instead.

If you're in a service business there's no need for you to pay to have your name professionally hand-painted in gold on your door. Go to a print shop or Staples and have them make up one of those neat black and white plastic name signs. By the time a client sees the name on your door he's already been sold.

Personally, I think the most effective marketing signage are those little roadside signs proclaiming that some business or organization has sponsored cleanup of that next two miles of highway. I don't know why, but even with all the huge billboards around overpowering them,

I always read those little sponsorship signs. Besides, if you change businesses in a year, yet continue to sponsor the cleanup, the state will pay for a new sign for you. That's kind of sign I like: effective, readily changeable, and free.

Speeches

Giving a speech is an excellent way to market yourself whether you're a mercenary employee or a Yourself.com entrepreneur. They're sort of the verbal equivalent of a magazine or journal article (see Chapter 55), setting you up as a well-respected, knowledgeable expert in your profession or industry.

Like articles, your speeches need to be polished. That means they require lot of preparation and attention to detail.

Be open to giving speeches in any forum. The more you practice the better you'll get, and the more often you speak the wider a net you're casting for future opportunities. That being said, industry- or association-sponsored conventions and seminars are the best forums for mercenary employees or Yourself.com entrepreneurs who sell to or service businesses, while adult educational forums—either formal classes or meeting of groups, clubs, or organizations—are best for Yourself.com entrepreneurs who sell to or service the general public.

Don't just write speeches, read them out loud. Often we say things much different from how we write them.* I've found that eloquence isn't as important as sincerity and passion.

Don't try to sell people on anything other than your ideas. Ironi-

---

*I learned this when I recorded the audio tape version of *Die Broke*. I found that phrases and words I had been comfortable with on the page just didn't flow coming out of my mouth.

cally, the less you directly promote yourself or your business, the better results you'll get from the speech. That's because once an audience member senses you're just up there trying to sell him, he loses respect for you and stops listening. And once you've lost him, you can't ever win him back.

Be as spontaneous and personable as you can. Try to frequently look up, smile, and make eye contact, even if you're reading. If you're afraid of speaking in public (it's a very common fear) consider taking a class or joining an organization like Toastmasters, which teaches you to write and present different kinds of speeches.

Always leave time for questions and answers. When it's time to start fielding queries step out from behind the podium and move toward the audience. You'll get more questions that way and people will be satisfied with more personal, less prepared answers.

Take a lesson from the chapters in the second half of this book. Keep things short and sweet. Fifteen minutes is plenty of time for most any subject—after all, the Gettysburg Address took less than five.

Spouse/Business and Career Conflicts   **88**

The whole point of becoming a mercenary employee or a Yourself.com entrepreneur is to live rich. And, for most of us, being able to spend more time with our families is a big part of living richer.

By eliminating many of the social and personal elements from your work life you will find you'll be able to do much more in the time you spend at work. You'll also no longer need to go to happy hour with the rest of the department, or take your boss out to dinner. That will in turn allow you to spend much more time at home or out with your family. As a result, mercenary employees and Yourself.com entrepreneurs will actually have far fewer family/business or career conflicts than others.

There's one catch, however. When you're at work you're working . . . hard . . . all the time. That means you're probably not going to be able to talk on the telephone with your spouse twice a day. You're not going to have the time to speak with your son when he calls the office from college, or stop what you're doing and take your daughter out for a long lunch when she surprises you with a visit. It's not just office socializing you're banishing from your work life, it's all socializing. If that ever causes a conflict just tell your family that focusing entirely at work while you're working lets you focus entirely on your family when you're home.

Stationery   **89**

I recently met a new Yourself.com entrepreneur client. He came to me for advice on expanding his market. He impressed me as an astute, dynamic, very creative fellow. At the conclusion of our meeting I asked him to send me a copy of his most recent marketing plan. When it arrived I was shocked. I couldn't believe this came from the same man I'd met. No, the plan was fine. Very polished, in fact. It was the stationery that didn't fit.

He was using a very common Macintosh font with a clip art logo on poor-quality colored paper he had purchased from one of those mail order paper catalogs. I told him his the first problem with his marketing plan was his stationery. He couldn't believe that was my most pressing criticism. "What about what I wrote?" he asked. I told him that didn't matter since I couldn't get past what the document looked like long enough to study it.

Obviously I was exaggerating. And after a couple of moments I told him so. But I had made my point. When you're in business for yourself your stationery is very important. And when you're a Yourself.com entrepreneur, with little or no staff or infrastructure to back you up, it's vital. Your letterhead is one of the first things some prospective clients and customers may see. It doesn't have to knock their socks off, but it must not do anything to turn them off. If there's anything disconcerting about it you're history.

Your stationery should be designed by the same professional who created your logo (see Chapter 54) and helped you put together your promotional kit (see Chapter 76). That designer needs to understand what you do and who you do it for. She must get an idea of the kind of image you want to create. Then she has to carry that image over onto every piece of paper you could possibly send to a client or customer.

Stationery with canned images, standard desktop publishing fonts, and obviously mass market designs say to the client or customer that you've no taste, no money, and/or no experience. They mark you as a fly-by-night amateur. Is that the image you want to put across?

You don't need to use very expensive papers or get fancy two-color printing jobs to have professional-looking stationery. All you need is to have a good, consistent, polished design that fits the nature of your business. And that design must be carried over from your letterhead to your envelopes, labels, fax cover sheets, and business cards.

As I told that new client, to live rich you need to have stationery that's as attractive and professional looking as you.

Suppliers and Vendors **90**

The last thing a Yourself.com retailer needs is a Yourself.com supplier. In this instance, throw solidarity out the window. You don't want someone with a streamlined operation telling you price and quality are what's important. You want someone who'll offer you soup to nuts service and hold your hand while providing it.

A Yourself.com retailer, whether he has his storefront in real space, cyberspace, or on paper, is not going to be able to provide the kind of lush experience many shoppers today crave. You won't have a huge inventory. You won't have a large, well-schooled staff of salespeople. In fact, you may not have any. You're not going to have extraordinary displays either. Instead, you need a supplier who'll provide you with all that kind of support, as well as with competitively priced, quality products.

You want a supplier who'll act as if he's your partner. He'll either provide you with drop shipping (you send him the order and he mails the product out to your customer direct) or just-in-time overnight delivery. He'll offer you all the sales information you could possibly want. Need text and photos for your Web site? He'll give you brochures to scan and a diskette with prescanned images. Need sales help and training? He'll give you self-promotion displays and videos to play in your store or on your Web site, and he'll send someone over to teach your part-timers about the merchandise. Worried about your opening day celebration? You need a supplier who'll run some co-op advertising for you, who'll provide you with free extra stock so your shelves look full, and who will split the cost of the pigs in a blanket. No Yourself.com could do any of that for you.

On the other hand, every Yourself.com entrepreneur would do better working with other Yourself.com vendors who provide the backroom services that keep the business running. You don't need to use a national chain to clean your offices, service your copiers, or print your stationery. You're looking for flexibility and sense of urgency, not state-of-the-art equipment or a basket at Christmas. All you need is one person who does a good job, on time, for a reasonable price, and who values your patronage. That sounds like a Yourself.com operation if you ask me.

Telephone Service Providers **91**

I get the feeling telephone service providers spend more time and money doing telemarketing and advertising than they do providing telephone service. Not a week goes by without my office getting a call encouraging us to switch. And not a night passes when I don't see some television commercial telling me what I'm paying for my long distance calls. And now, with local service being deregulated, it's going to get even crazier. What's a Yourself.com entrepreneur to do? Well, one thing you can do is take advantage of it.

It takes no time or energy on your part to switch telephone service providers. And since you keep the same telephones, telephone number, and in most cases, central equipment, the only differences will be your costs and where you send your check each month. It appears that there's no clear low-cost provider—it varies based on your location and the types of calls you make. Therefore, it pays to shop around.

The next time you get one of those annoying calls, explain the types of calls you make and get a promise from a provider that your rates will drop. Tell them you'll switch if they pick up the cost (they all will). If your costs drop in the first month, great. If not, call and ask what happened. Say you'll switch if you don't see savings in the next month. Act on your threat, and then keep switching until you find someone whose rates cannot be beaten.

If that sounds like the kind of shopping experience you'd like to avoid, why not sign up with Working Assets Long Distance (1-800-548-2567)? It's a not-for-profit service that donates a portion of its proceeds to charities selected by the customers.

The service is fine, the rates are competitive, and you'll be doing something for your community.

Temps

92

Temps are fabulous resources for a Yourself.com entrepreneur. I think of them as just-in-time employees.

Temps provide the ultimate flexibility. You can hire them for as long or as short as you need. It could be for a project that lasts one day, one week, one month, or one year, offering you the ability to change on a dime, or expand and contract operations, without worrying about having to hire and/or terminate.

Temps can come in early in the morning, late at night, or on weekends, allowing you to work on multiple businesses simultaneously. You could run one business with a regular staff during normal business hours, and then have your second operation running at night or on the weekend with temps.

If you work through a good agency you know you'll be getting someone who's competent, courteous, and well-dressed. Take it from me, that's not a given if you hire on your own. Unless they're on site for more than a month or two, temps won't get involved in any kind of office politics. Knowing they're not long for the company they keep a low profile, do their job, check the classified ads, and go home. That's my idea of a dream employee.

You can use your temps as a resource pool. Having found a couple of good temps you can request them again in the future, turning them into quasi vendors. In my office we keep a list of half a dozen temps we've been pleased with and what their best traits were. That way, when we know we'll need a temporary receptionist in August, we can call ahead of time and "reserve" a particular temp.

Finally, you can use temps as a pool from which to draw full-time employees. While most like the flexibility temping offers them, quite a few temps are actually looking to land full-time jobs. Most agency agreements contain a clause requiring you to pay a set amount if you do eventually hire a temp as an employee. However, in my experience that fee is no greater than what you'd pay hiring through an employment agency. And in the case of a temp you're hiring a known quantity.

There are three downsides to using temps. First, they're not going to be familiar with your business's culture. Second, they may require more hands-on managing than regular employees. And third, they can be a security risk. In my office we've dealt with these problems in a number of ways.

We've prepared a standard sheet of instructions for our temps. This is the first thing temps are handed on their first day, and to impress them with the importance of it they're asked to sign it after reading. Here's a slightly edited version of our instruction sheet:

> Welcome. Here are a few things you may need to know about the office. We will all be happy to explain anything further or answer any questions not covered.

> ### GENERAL

> Try to listen for the doorbell and answer the door quickly, since we don't like to have people waiting in the hall.

> Please ask all visitors, including messengers and delivery people, to step into the office instead of standing in the hall.

> If you're on the telephone someone else will get the door.

> When messengers pick up deliveries, ask for a receipt.

> When clients arrive, greet them at the door. Introduce yourself and ask for their name. Help them with their coats, umbrellas, etc. Direct them to the waiting area. Offer them coffee (decaffeinated or caffeinated), tea, or water. Show them where the rest room is. Tell them "Stephen" (not "Mr. Pollan") will be out to see

them shortly. If they are a new client, give them a Client Contact Sheet attached to the clipboard on top of the cabinet nearest the door and ask them to fill it out.

Tell Stephen his next appointment is here. If his door is shut simply knock before you enter.

After the meeting give the completed Client Contact Sheet to Anthony so he can start a new file.

We play classical CDs throughout the day. Please try to change them periodically (choose any you like), since they can get repetitive very quickly.

Keep track of the supply of milk and other foodstuffs in the refrigerator. If you notice we're running low tell Anthony or place an order at East Side Bagels.

If you find we're running low of office supplies tell Anthony so he can place an order.

TELEPHONES

We answer the telephone "Stephen Pollan's office."

Record Stephen's incoming calls on the call list. Always be sure to get telephone numbers and try to get a message too.

Stephen will tell you which outgoing calls he wishes to make each day.

At the end of the day go over the call list to see who Stephen didn't have time to speak with and add them to the call list for the next day. Also make note of people who haven't yet returned Stephen's calls.

Messages for everyone else should go on message slips.

The answering machine will pick up if calls aren't answered promptly, so everyone pitches in to get the telephone when it rings.

Try not to keep anyone on hold for very long. If the person they're holding for doesn't pick up right away, ask the caller if they want to continue to hold or would like to leave a message.

We keep logs for the fax machine. For incoming faxes, please note the client's name or office or book project on the incoming fax log. For outgoing faxes, write the client's name or office or book project on the back of the cover sheet.

FIRST THING IN THE MORNING

Turn on the air conditioning and lights.

Check the answering machine and record all messages.

Turn on the photocopier and printers.

Change the date on the postage meter.

Turn on the stereo.

Turn on all the computers and open the diary/contact software.

Turn on the fish tank light and feed the fish (instructions on tank).

Update and distribute the appointment schedule.

COMPUTERS

The computers in the office are on a network so you can work from anyone's computer. To connect to someone else's hard drive, select "chooser" under the apple menu,* and then select "share."

Any computer question that can't be answered internally should be addressed to Peter Donleavy at (212) 555–1212.

Always write interview information in the office diary.

MAILING LISTS

Various mailing lists can be created from the Rolodex by highlighting the keyword. Many of these have form letters attached.

---

*On a Macintosh, the first menu item on the desktop doesn't have a name. Instead there's a picture of an apple.

TRAVEL SCHEDULING

For domestic travel Stephen uses GoUSA at (212) 555–1313.

For international travel Stephen uses GoWorld at (212) 555–1414.

We try to overcome the management problem by asking temps to do only fairly rote work, nothing that requires an in-depth knowledge of our business or clients. On their first morning they're given the sheet of instructions, we explain the culture of our office, spell out what kind of behavior we expect, and describe how we want our clients treated. Their work is reviewed one hour after they start, then again prior to their lunch break, and finally before they leave at the end of the day. On their second day they're again given instructions, but their work is reviewed only twice: before lunch and then at the end of the day. If they haven't caught on by the end of the second day we ask for another temp. If they have learned the ropes, on their third and subsequent days their work is reviewed only at the end of the day.

We deal with the secrecy, or in the case of our office, privacy issue directly. On their first day we tell the temp that one of the reasons clients use our services is that we offer them a great deal of privacy. We stress that what goes on in the office stays in the office. However, we don't leave things to chance. Our active management helps, but so does giving very sensitive computer files a password and storing certain papers in a locked filing cabinet. Since I make it a practice to hold sensitive conversations in my office with the door closed, we're not too worried about what a temp overhears.

Terminations

93

Terminations are going to get a lot easier to handle, from both sides of the desk. No, I haven't come up with a magic termination formula for either mercenary employees or Yourself.com entrepreneurs. It's just that the more common something becomes, the less stigma is attached to it and the less traumatic it becomes. Terminations are today a fact of life for both mercenary employees and Yourself.com entrepreneurs. And they're going to be even more common in the future.

No employer can guarantee an employee job security regardless of his performance. Yourself.com entrepreneurs, who run tighter operations than traditional businesses and who need to respond instantly to any change in profitability, can barely guarantee next month's paycheck, let alone long-term security. That means every Yourself.com entrepreneur needs to become an expert terminator.

Warmth and compassion are noble emotions, but when it comes to termination they're a mistake. I know it's not pleasant, but you must think of yourself like a butcher. Your job is to slaughter, but to do so quickly and cleanly, inflicting the minimum pain and leaving little mess to clean up.

Speak to your attorney to establish a litigation-proof termination process and a set of documents. The process will probably involve at least three steps combining both verbal meetings and written documentation of the specifics: a performance review, a formal warning, and a termination meeting.

For the sake of the employee (and your own legal bills) you must be clear and unambiguous throughout. Better to be blunt and risk appearing cold than to be warm and risk a misunderstanding that results in your getting sued. You must directly tell the employee that he's going to lose his job unless his behavior changes, his performance improves, or the company's finances pick up, within a specified period of time. Halfway to that deadline you must restate the facts, putting him on notice of his impending termination. Then, on the date selected, you must terminate him.

The termination meeting should be formal and ritualized. It's better to terminate someone as early in the day and as early in the week as possible. That gives the employee a chance to act on his future the rest of the day and week, rather than dwell on his past. Be clear, direct, and uncompromising. You can be sympathetic, but do not offer any hope. There's no room for compromise and no going back. Have a closure document, already prepared by your lawyer, ready for him to sign. Have a letter of reference already prepared. And have his severance check already made out as well. Unless you've previously agreed to an amount, or it would be a financial hardship for the business, it should be for at least two weeks' pay for every year he's been your employee. Do not negotiate the amount. Do not negotiate any extra time either. The employee must leave today. If he wants to get the check and the positive reference letter to take with him, he has to sign the release. There's no room for discussion.

You need to face the facts. If you're going to hire people, as sure as night follows day, you're also going to have to fire people. Don't procrastinate or lose sleep over it. Just do it so they can move on with their life and you can move on with your work.

Mercenary employees need to be just as cold and calculating about terminations. In fact, I'd suggest that if you end up being terminated it's partly your own fault. You should have seen the financial trouble or performance problems coming and gotten out of there before it came to this. In fact, I tell all my mercenary employee clients to launch a pre-emptive strike if they think they're in trouble at work. Go in to your superior and ask whether your suspicions or perceptions are justified. If he says no, don't feel safe, just get it in writing and accept that his denial gives you some additional leverage when the ax does fall. If he says yes, ask what you can do about it. Get his response in writing, and do all you can to respond . . . while looking for another job. Once again, you're just increasing your leverage.

Leverage really is the key for mercenary employees about to be terminated. Your goal isn't to keep your job—if they don't want you, you don't want to be there—your goal is to get as much severance as possible. Your having a written statement denying your job was in danger, or a document outlining what you could do to save your job, can only help your negotiating position. In addition, your being a member of any protected group—whether based on gender, race, religion, national origin, sexual preference, age, long-term employment, or physical ability—might offer implicit leverage.

If you don't have any of any of these types of leverage you should still try to negotiate for more severance, continued use of the facilities, and anything else you can think of. However, if your former employer sticks to his guns, take the money, sign the release, and get the heck out of there. The sooner this is behind you, the better.

If you do have leverage, refuse to sign anything without first speaking to your attorney. Ask for a meeting for the next morning. Get up and leave the check on the table. Trust me. If you have leverage it will still be there tomorrow, and besides, you might be able to get them to tear it up and write a bigger one. With or without an attorney's help, draft a memo outlining your dream severance package. Present it at your next meeting as if you were never even offered anything else. Then start horse trading. Obviously you want to get as much as you can, but you also want to get this all behind you as soon as possible.

Bear in mind that your employer wants you out of there and needs your signature on that release. You've never been as powerful in your negotiation with him. What more can he do to you? He's already fired you.

94

Make the most from every moment you're working and you'll make more money and have more time to live rich.

Everyone has to develop an individual time management system. Some people like using desk diaries, others rely on to-do lists, and some use contact management software. No one product or system is better than any other. Whatever works, works.

That being said, there are some general rules I'd encourage you to follow.

First, plan as much of your day and week as possible so you're spending uninterrupted time working. There will always be some emergencies and valid interruptions, but the more planning you do the easier it will be keep to a schedule.

Second, start early (see Chapter 78). I'm not the only Yourself.com entrepreneur who has found that the most productive hours of the day are those before the telephone starts ringing and before the staff arrives.

Third, make prioritized lists of what you need to accomplish and tackle the most difficult tasks first. For years, when facing a task I thought would be difficult or unpleasant, I procrastinated. But the task never went away as I wished it would. In fact, the longer I waited to do it, the more terrifying it became. Once I realized that, I changed patterns and started tackling the thing I least wanted to do first. Incredibly, these distasteful tasks now never seem to be as bad as I anticipate.

Whether that's because I have less time to worry or I'm just fooling myself doesn't really matter. What counts is that I'm now getting more done.

Fourth, return every call within twenty-four hours. I make sure that either I or a member of my staff returns every single call that comes into the office. (My office averages fifty incoming calls a day.) Many days I spend my last half-hour in the office placing dozens of calls and leaving many messages on answering machines. It doesn't take a lot of effort and it reaps incredible goodwill.*

Fifth, and last, try to be as realistic as possible when calculating delivery times and deadlines, and let clients and customers know as early as possible if schedules need to change. No client ever calls my office to ask why he didn't get something on time. That's because I never set a deadline; I offer conditional estimates. For instance I'll say that if everything goes according to plan we should be ready around Thursday. Then, if anything happens that wasn't planned, I call right away, explain what has happened, and offer a new conditional estimate. As a result, I can honestly say my office has never missed a deadline.

---

*While I think everyone will gain by returning calls promptly, I think I gain more than most. That's because I'm an attorney and no professionals have a worse reputation for returning calls than lawyers. When a client gets a call back from a lawyer within twenty-four hours he really sits up and takes notice.

95

My feelings about business travel have come full circle.

When I was first starting out in business I loved it. It was exciting to hop a plane, check into a hotel, and visit a client or go to a convention. I'd get to fly, stay in nice hotels, and dine in fancy restaurants. Out on the road I felt like a successful executive, regardless of what my bottom line looked like.

Then, as I got older, I started to really hate business travel. Planes were uncomfortable, hotels all looked the same, and dining out got passé. Travel meant time away from my family; away from the life I wanted to be living.

But a couple of years ago my feelings changed yet again. It's not that I've suddenly rekindled my love of airport lounges and room service coffee. It's that I've learned to use travel as an opportunity to get more work done.

Now, when I know I'm going to be flying somewhere, I spend the previous week setting aside work I can do on the flight and at the hotel.* I make sure to upgrade my ticket from coach to business class, and turn my seat into a cocoon of an office. Because I'm out of touch with my office I can actually accomplish as much reading and writing

---

*I never plan on doing any work while driving. My wife doesn't even like me to talk when I'm behind the wheel.

on a three-hour flight as I would in three normal days in the office. When my flight lands I feel like I've really accomplished something.

Sure, the upgrade is costly. But if I'm attending to a client's business I can bill for the hours of prep work I'm doing on the flight. (I never bill for time spent on return flights, by the way.) Even if I'm not on a specific project, the work I accomplish on the flight translates into my having more billable hours when I return to the office. I simply multiply my hourly fee by the length of the flight. If that adds up to more than the cost of upgrading, I do it.

I always arrive the night before a meeting so I can be fresh the next day. I look for a hotel as close to the site of my meeting as possible so I can spend more time the next morning preparing than traveling. As soon as I check into the hotel I arrange to have my clothing for the meeting day pressed. I familiarize myself with the telephone system so I don't end up getting charged $10 for a local call. I arrange for breakfast and a newspaper to be delivered to my room the next morning. Then I go to bed early.

On the day of the meeting I wake up early. I have a leisurely breakfast in my room, read the newspaper, and watch a little of the morning news on television. I call the front desk to arrange for a cab. After I've showered and dressed I pack. Then I do my premeeting prep work. I go downstairs early, check out, and jump in the cab to head to the meeting.

Once the meeting ends I ask to use a telephone. I first call to make sure my flight is on time. I next call for a cab to take me to the airport. Finally, I call my office to check in. On the flight back I conduct a postmortem of the meeting in my head, read any material I've been given, and compose any correspondence I'll be sending out as a result of the meeting. However the meeting went, I now always arrive home feeling as if I've accomplished something . . . because I have.

Web Sites

96

I was never a big believer in entrepreneurs designing their own stores. Sure, as long as a customer can see and evaluate a product he might buy it. But if there are other stores selling similar products displayed in a much more appealing manner, the customer will certainly shop and probably buy from the better-designed shop.

I'm against Yourself.com entrepreneurs designing their own Web sites for the same reason. Customers and clients will come back to and shop from your Web page only if it's well-designed. And that requires a professional.

That doesn't mean you have no role in the process. Your job is to explain the nature of your business and your goals. The designer's job is to use your explanations to drive the design of the site.

The single most important goal is that your Web site be easy to use. It's just like a store. If customers can't find what they want quickly and easily, they'll leave and never come back. That means your business name and your product or service must be instantly apparent—just as if you had a sign.

Your site must be well-organized. It must have the right number of pages, linked together in a rational manner. A well-organized site is also easy to navigate. Your home page not only should be attractive, but also should give visitors an overview of the whole site and help them decide where to go next to accomplish their goal.

Your content should be direct and to the point. If you wouldn't have a twenty-foot-high blinking neon sign outside your business in the real world, then there's certainly no reason to have a rotating flaming logo in cyberspace either. Another reason to keep it direct is to save time. Fancy graphics take a long time to download. If your customers have to wait too long they'll lose interest and go elsewhere.

Pages should be designed to fit the screen sizes most customers or clients use: twelve to fourteen inches or 640 pixels wide by 480 pixels high. Anything larger will frustrate visitors and they'll soon leave.

Images and graphics should enhance, not dominate, your Web site. Words are still the primary means of communication. If an image or graphic doesn't serve a specific purpose that words cannot, don't use it. It just takes up space on your site and increases download time.

While the Web is a new environment the rules of written communication haven't gone out the window. In fact, if anything, they're more important on the Web than anywhere else. That means all your prose should be concise, grammatical, and properly spelled. If you need to hire an editor to ensure that's the case, do so.

Don't forget that if your customers can't read your information, they're not likely to do business with you. Stick to black text on a white background for the bulk of your copy. Use serif typefaces—they're easier to read—and font sizes that are easily seen. Work in small blocks of text so the words don't run either across an entire page or from one screen to another.

Since you're not there behind the counter of the cybershop to field questions you must provide your visitors with some kind of interactivity. It could be as simple as an e-mail link so customers can contact you. It could also be a cyber "guestbook" in which people can leave their names, e-mail addresses, and comments. If your site is large enough that a customer could get lost, it should have some kind of search tool ranging from a simple map to a keyword search tool. You wouldn't leave a customer alone in your store, so don't leave him alone on your Web site.

Word of Mouth

97

Every marketing expert will tell you there's nothing better than word-of-mouth advertising. In the next breath they'll say, "Too bad it can't be bought," and will move on to selling you on other techniques that can be bought . . . from them.

Those experts are right on both counts. Word of mouth is the best form of marketing, and it cannot be bought. But that doesn't mean you can't solicit it.

As a mercenary employee or Yourself.com entrepreneur you'll have much closer relations with clients, customers, and contacts than the average individual. They'll know you care about them and will feel they can trust you. Now you need to trust them. Set aside some of your pride. Whenever you receive a compliment from clients or customers, thank them first, but then ask them to spread the word about you. Ask them to tell your superiors about your excellent customer service, their friends about what a great job you did for them, or their family about how wonderful your products are.

If it's appropriate, consider offering referral discounts or bonuses. At the very least, ask new clients or customers who referred them, and then send a thank-you note to your supporter.

Post a sign or add a paragraph to your promotional brochure encouraging customers with complaints to voice them to you, and customers with compliments to voice them to a friend.

Once I set aside my foolish pride and starting asking my clients to recommend me to their family and friends, I made an interesting discovery. My existing clients liked doing it. It seemed to make them feel like they were trendsetters: They were doing their friends a favor by introducing them to a special club. Asking them to refer my practice to others has made them feel closer to both me and my office; they're taking pride in our success. When your clients or customers start acting like partners you're well on the road to living rich.

Working Capital

98

Yourself.com entrepreneurs, like most small business people, are apt to suffer from cash flow problems leading to working capital shortages. In plain English: There will probably be a time you don't have enough cash to pay your bills.

There are a number of ways around this common problem. First, make sure you have sufficient capital in the first place. That's unlikely, since almost every start-up is undercapitalized. Second, plan carefully. Know when you're apt to have large bills to pay and when you're going to be short of cash, and compensate for it. Third, watch your receivables (see Chapter 80) and payables (see Chapter 69) like a hawk. And fourth, get yourself some unused credit.*

When you're flush with funds, head over to that local bank that refused to loan you seed money. Either obtain a line of credit or get a credit card with as large a limit as possible. Since you don't need the money the bank is sure to lend it to you. Because this is only for emergencies, don't shy away from taking it out with your personal credit. Then, every six months or so, take a small advance and quickly pay it off to keep the credit line active. Otherwise, forget it exists. In fact, keep the card or checkbook locked away somewhere that's inconvenient.

*Before you apply for more credit, be sure to first check your credit file. You don't want to be turned down.

The next time you're faced with a working capital shortage—say you need to make an estimated tax payment but haven't received your payment from a big customer—simply tap into your unused credit. As soon as the payment comes in, pay off your credit line and lock the checkbook away again.

Appendix:
Sources for More Information

As I'm sure you know there are thousands of books on career and small business issues. Most offer conventional advice that runs counter to the Live Rich approach. However, there are some excellent works that, while their authors may not agree with my philosophy, offer information that has helped my clients and me in our efforts to live rich. This is a highly subjective list. It's intended solely to help you get started. As you might imagine from reading all the previous chapters, the list for entrepreneurs is heavily weighted toward books on marketing, and the list for employees doesn't offer much guidance about skydiving. So if you need more help or want a more conventional approach, speak to a good reference librarian. If that's not sufficient, just give me a call.

FOR YOURSELF.COM ENTREPRENEURS

Do-It-Yourself Direct Marketing Secrets for Small Business by Mark S. Bacon.

Getting Business to Come to You by Paul Edwards, Sarah Edwards, and Laura Clampit Douglas.

Guerrilla Advertising by Jay Conrad Levinson.

Guerrilla Marketing Attack by Jay Conrad Levinson.

Guerrilla Selling by Jay Conrad Levinson, Bill Gallagher, and Orvel Ray Wilson.

How to Promote, Publicize, and Advertise Your Growing Business: Getting the Word Out Without Spending a Fortune by Kim Baker and Sunny Baker.

Inc. Yourself: How to Profit by Setting Up Your Own Corporation by Judith H. McQuown.

Marketing on a Shoestring by Jeff Davidson.

Marketing Without Advertising by Michael Philips and Salli Rasberry.

1,001 Ideas to Create Retail Excitement by Edgar A. Falk.

The Portable MBA in Entrepreneurship, edited by William D. Bygrave.

Small Business Management: A Guide to Entrepreneurship by Nicholas Siropolis.

Small Business Management: An Entrepreneurial Emphasis by Justin G. Longenecker, Carlos W. Moore, and J. William Petty.

Small Business Trends and Entrepreneurship: How Entrepreneurs Are Reshaping the Economy and What You Can Learn from Them by the editors of *Business Week.*

Start Your Own Business for $1,000 or Less by Will Davis.

Starting and Managing the Small Business by Arthur H. Kuriloff, John M. Hemphill, Jr., and Douglas Cloud.

Starting on a Shoestring: Building a Business Without a Bankroll by Arnold S. Goldstein.

Target Smart: Database Marketing for the Small Business by Jay Newberg and Claudio Marcus.

Teaming Up: The Small Business Guide to Collaborating with Others to Boost Your Earnings and Expand Your Horizons by Paul Edwards, Sarah Edwards, and Rick Benzel.

Working from Home by Paul Edwards and Sarah Edwards.

Working Solo by Terri Lonier.

Working Solo Sourcebook by Terri Lonier.

FOR MERCENARY EMPLOYEES

The Age of Unreason by Charles Handy.

Creating You & Co.: Learn to Think Like the CEO of Your Own Career by William Bridges.

Fast Company. I've been quite impressed by this new monthly magazine. I'm taking a bit of a risk listing it here because you never know how long a new periodical will last. However, I've been struck by how well the editors of this magazine have tapped into the needs and spirit of the mercenary employee. I highly recommend it.

From Chaos to Confidence: Survival Strategies for the New Workplace by Susan M. Campbell.

How to Fireproof Your Career: Survival Strategies for Volatile Times by Anne Baber and Lynne Waymon.

Job Shift: How to Prosper in a Workplace Without Jobs by William Bridges.

The Longevity Factor: The New Reality of Long Careers and How It Can Lead to Richer Lives by Lydia Brontë.

Marketing Yourself: The Ultimate Job Seeker's Guide by Dorothy Leeds.

The New Rules: Eight Business Breakthroughs to Career Success in the 21st Century by John P. Kotter.

Outplace Yourself: Secrets of an Executive Outplacement Counselor by Charles H. Logue.

Index